P9-DNM-109

0000   6934

S   E   R   I   E   S

A NavPress Bible study on the book of

REVELATION

NAVPRESS

NAVPRESS⬤.

Navpress is the publishing ministry of The Navigators, an international Christian organization and leader in personal spiritual development. NavPress is committed to helping people grow spiritually and enjoy lives of meaning and hope through personal and group resources that are biblically rooted, culturally relevant, and highly practical.

For a free catalog go to www.NavPress.com
or call 1.800.366.7788 in the United States or 1.800.839.4769 in Canada.

NAVPRESS, and the NAVPRESS logo are registered trademarks of NavPress. Absence of ® in connection with marks of NavPress or other parties does not indicate an absence of registration of those marks.

www.navpress.com

ISBN 978-0-89109-273-5

Most Scripture quotations are from the *Holy Bible: New International Version* (NIV). Copyright © 1973, 1978, 1984, International Bible Society. Used by permission of Zondervan Bible Publishers. Other versions used are the *New American Standard Bible* (NASB), © The Lockman Foundation 1960, 1962, 1963, 1968, 1971, 1972, 1973, 1975, 1977; and the *King James Version* (KJV).

Printed in the United States of America

23 24 25 26 27 28 / 14 13 12 11 10 09 08

CONTENTS

ACKNOWLEDGMENTS

The LIFECHANGE series has been produced through the coordinated efforts of a team of Navigator Bible study developers and NavPress editorial staff, along with a nationwide network of fieldtesters.

SERIES EDITOR: KAREN LEE-THORP

HOW TO USE THIS STUDY

Objectives

Most guides in the LIFECHANGE series of Bible studies cover one book of the Bible. Although the LIFECHANGE guides vary with the books they explore, they share some common goals:

1. To provide you with a firm foundation of understanding and a thirst to return to the book;

2. To teach you by example how to study a book of the Bible without structured guides;

3. To give you all the historical background, word definitions, and explanatory notes you need, so that your only other reference is the Bible;

4. To help you grasp the message of the book as a whole;

5. To teach you how to let God's Word transform you into Christ's image.

Each lesson in this study is designed to take 60 to 90 minutes to complete on your own. The guide is based on the assumption that you are completing one lesson per week, but if time is limited you can do half a lesson per week or whatever amount allows you to be thorough.

Flexibility

LIFECHANGE guides are flexible, allowing you to adjust the quantity and depth of your study to meet your individual needs. The guide offers many optional questions in addition to the regular numbered questions. The optional questions, which appear in the margins of the study pages, include the following:

Optional Application. Nearly all application questions are optional; we hope you will do as many as you can without overcommitting yourself.

For Thought and Discussion. Beginning Bible students should be able to handle these, but even advanced students need to think about them. These questions frequently deal with ethical issues and other biblical principles. They often offer cross-references to spark thought, but the references do not give

5

obvious answers. They are good for group discussions.

For Further Study. These include: a) cross-references that shed light on a topic the book discusses, and b) questions that delve deeper into the passage. You can omit them to shorten a lesson without missing a major point of the passage.

If you are meeting in a group, decide together which optional questions to prepare for each lesson, and how much of the lesson you will cover at the next meeting. Normally, the group leader should make this decision, but you might let each member choose his or her own application questions.

As you grow in your walk with God, you will find the LIFECHANGE guide growing with you—a helpful reference on a topic, a continuing challenge for application, a source of questions for many levels of growth.

Overview and Details

The study begins with an overview of the book of Revelation. The key to interpretation is context—what is the whole passage or book *about?*—and the key to context is purpose—what is the author's *aim* for the whole work? In lesson one you will lay the foundation for your study of Revelation by asking yourself, "Why did the author (and God) write the book? What did they want to accomplish? What is the book about?"

In lessons two through fourteen you will analyze successive passages of Revelation in detail.

In lesson fifteen you will review Revelation, returning to the big picture to see whether your view of it has changed after closer study. Review will also strengthen your grasp of major issues and give you an idea of how you have grown from your study.

Kinds of Questions

Bible study on your own—without a structured guide—follows a progression. First you observe: What does the passage *say*? Then you interpret: What does the passage *mean*? Lastly you apply: How does this truth *affect* my life?

Some of the "how" and "why" questions will take some creative thinking, even prayer, to answer. Some are opinion questions without clear-cut right answers; these will lend themselves to discussions and side studies.

Don't let your study become an exercise of knowledge alone. Treat the passage as God's Word, and stay in dialogue with Him as you study. Pray, "Lord, what do You want me to see here?" "Father, why is this true?" "Lord, how does this apply to my life?"

It is important that you write down your answers. The act of writing clarifies your thinking and helps you to remember.

Study Aids

A list of reference materials, including a few notes of explanation to help you make good use of them, begins on page 163. This guide is designed to include enough background to let you interpret with just your Bible and the guide. Still, if you want more information on a subject or want to study a book on your own, try the references listed.

Scripture Versions

Unless otherwise indicated, the Bible quotations in this guide are from the New International Version of the Bible. Other versions cited are the New American Standard Bible (NASB) and the King James Version (KJV).

Use any translation you like for study, preferably more than one. A paraphrase such as The Living Bible is not accurate enough for study, but it can be helpful for comparison or devotional reading.

Memorizing and Meditating

A psalmist wrote, "I have hidden your word in my heart that I might not sin against you" (Psalm 119:11). If you write down a verse or passage that challenges or encourages you, and reflect on it often for a week or more, you will find it beginning to affect your motives and actions. We forget quickly what we read once; we remember what we ponder.

When you find a significant verse or passage, you might copy it onto a card to keep with you. Set aside five minutes during each day just to think about what the passage might mean in your life. Recite it over to yourself, exploring its meaning. Then, return to your passage as often as you can during your day, for a brief review. You will soon find it coming to mind spontaneously.

For Group Study

A group of four to ten people allows the richest discussions, but you can adapt this guide for other sized groups. It will suit a wide range of group types, such as home Bible studies, growth groups, youth groups, and businessmen's studies. Both new and experienced Bible students, and new and mature Christians, will benefit from the guide. You can omit or leave for later years any questions you find too easy or too hard.

The guide is intended to lead a group through one lesson per week. However, feel free to split lessons if you want to discuss them more thoroughly. Or, omit some questions in a lesson if preparation or discussion time is limited. You can always return to this guide for personal study later. You will be able to discuss only a few questions at length, so choose some for discussion and others for background. Make time at each discussion for

7

members to ask about anything they didn't understand.

Each lesson in the guide ends with a section called "For the group." These sections give advice on how to focus a discussion, how you might apply the lesson in your group, how you might shorten a lesson, and so on. The group leader should read each "For the group" at least a week ahead so that he or she can tell the group how to prepare for the next lesson.

Each member should prepare for a meeting by writing answers for all of the background and discussion questions to be covered. If the group decides not to take an hour per week for private preparation, then expect to take at least two meetings per lesson to work through the questions. Application will be very difficult, however, without private thought and prayer.

Two reasons for studying in a group are accountability and support. When each member commits in front of the rest to seek growth in an area of life, you can pray with one another, listen jointly for God's guidance, help one another to resist temptation, assure each other that the other's growth matters to you, use the group to practice spiritual principles, and so on. Pray about one another's commitments and needs at most meetings. Spend the first few minutes of each meeting sharing any results from applications prompted by previous lessons. Then discuss new applications toward the end of the meeting. Follow such sharing with prayer for these and other needs.

If you write down each other's applications and prayer requests, you are more likely to remember to pray for them during the week, ask about them at the next meeting, and notice answered prayers. You might want to get a notebook for prayer requests and discussion notes.

Notes taken during discussion will help you to remember, follow up on ideas, stay on the subject, and clarify a total view of an issue. But don't let note-taking keep you from participating. Some groups choose one member at each meeting to take notes. Then someone copies the notes and distributes them at the next meeting. Rotating these tasks can help include people. Some groups have someone take notes on a large pad of paper or erasable marker board (preformed shower wallboard works well), so that everyone can see what has been recorded.

Pages 166-167 list some good sources of counsel for leading group studies. The *Small Group Letter,* published by NavPress, is unique, offering insights from experienced leaders every other month.

LESSON ONE

OVERVIEW

The Revelation

Map of Asia

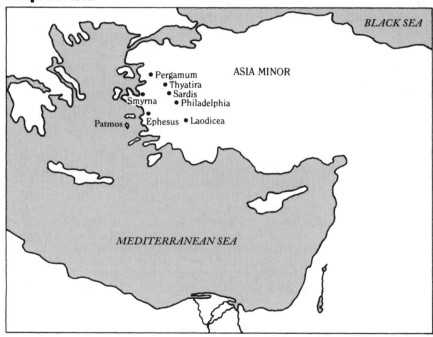

Jesus' resurrection was about sixty-five years ago. Most of the people who knew Him personally are dead, and a second generation of Christians has grown up. The gospel asserts that Jesus is King of the world and is coming back soon to claim His domain. But the years pass, and still He does not come. Now a madman has become emperor of Rome who actually believes the poets' praises that he is a god incarnate. He likes to be addressed as "Our Lord and God."[1] He has decreed that anyone who holds public office, anyone who testifies in court—practically everyone—must offer a pinch of incense to the emperor's guardian spirit and declare "Caesar is Lord." If a person refuses to worship the emperor, he may lose his job, his home, even his life.

9

This is not the only threat to Christians in 95 AD. Within the churches are some members who want to take control and twist the gospel to suit themselves. Danger without and danger within—*is God really in control?* In part to answer this question for embattled Christians in the first century and every century since, God gave a series of visions to someone named John. It is called "The revelation of Jesus Christ, which God gave him to show his servants what must soon take place" (Revelation 1:1).

Controversy and agreement

The book of Revelation was not written as a riddle for well-fed Christians to amuse themselves with. Rather, it was given for believers under a lot of pressure from the state, religious institutions, the economy, and even their fellow church members. It was not meant to be so difficult that ordinary Christians would be afraid to study and apply it for themselves without an authority to explain the puzzle. In fact, it is the only book of the Bible that states an explicit blessing just for reading it (1:3) and another for acting on it (22:7)! If God expects believers to read, take to heart, and apply the Revelation to their lives, then He must not have intended it to be a closed book. And indeed, although Bible-believing Christians differ widely on how to interpret many of the book's details, they agree on many of its main issues and applications for today.

If you've been in Christian circles awhile, you've probably heard people talk about "the millenium," "the rapture," "the beast," and "666." Since the LIFECHANGE series is intended to help you discover the truths of Scripture for yourself, we will try to let you make up your own mind about these things. We will not attempt to interpret every detail of the visions; the commentaries on pages 163-164 do an excellent job of this from a variety of viewpoints. But we will try to outline some of the major approaches to different passages, giving you the benefits of several views. You will find references to the first-century setting to help you understand how John's first readers would have understood his visions. You will also find questions that ask what a passage tells you about the end times. (We'll leave it to you to decide whether "the end times" are the last years before the Second Coming, or all of history since the Resurrection, or both.)

Our focus will always be on how you should respond to what the book says: "Blessed is he who keeps [acts on] the words of the prophecy in this book" (22:7). We will be less concerned with the precise meaning of each symbol than with the timeless truths you learn and how they are relevant to your life. In most cases, the present applications of the book are the same whatever you conclude about predictions of the future.

One of the reasons Revelation seems so difficult to modern readers is that it draws heavily upon images of nearly every book of the Old Testament (and several of the New). In fact, Revelation has been described as a lens that draws together and brings into focus the whole rest of the Bible. The notes in each lesson will explain many of these biblical references and suggest others for you to pursue if you want to delve deeper.

10

Themes

Christians of many viewpoints agree on these great issues of the book:

God—His character, nature, and attributes. How can Revelation help us
know, love, trust, and obey Him better?
Christ—His work and its results. How can Revelation help us know Him
better?
Ultimate reality—What is the universe's true meaning and purpose?
Power—Who has it, and who only seems to?
Evil—Its source and nature. Why do Christians suffer?
The Kingdom of God—What is it really about?
Our response—How should Christians respond to their situations in light of
these truths?

Apocalypse

John calls his book "The revelation of Jesus Christ" (1:1). The word "revelation" is *apokalypsis* in Greek, which means "unveiling" or "disclosure."
John's book records the unveiling of the goals and truths of history. Because
Revelation is similar to a whole genre of Jewish literature written between
200 BC and 100 AD, modern scholars call that genre "apocalyptic." If we
compare the Revelation to other apocalypses, we can see some similarities
that help us understand what John was doing, as well as some crucial differences that set his work apart.[2]

In general, an apocalypse purports to be a revelation from God through
a heavenly intermediary (such as an angel) to a great figure of the past (like
Moses or Enoch). The message often uses gripping symbolism to show that
God will intervene in history to bring evil to an end. The latter half of the
book of Daniel is the model for this genre. But the apocalyptic form became
popular several centuries after Daniel, when Israel ceased to have living
prophets to speak God's current word. The people needed to understand what
God was doing when the voice of the prophets was silent and the nation's
suffering was intense.

In fact, apocalypse has been called "the child of prophecy."[3] The
prophets did use highly colored language to describe the coming day of the
Lord and the Kingdom of God (Isaiah 35:1-10, Amos 9:11-15, Micah 1:4), and
these visions are the seeds of apocalypse. Yet there are differences. First,
while prophecy was oral preaching later written down, apocalypses were
literature from the beginning. Second, the prophets were concerned with
ethics, how people should act alongside God in resisting evil. The apocalyptists did not discuss ethics, for they believed that nothing short of divine
intervention could do anything about the world's evil. Third, while the
prophets usually spoke to their contemporaries and saw the end of the world
as somewhat more distant, the apocalyptists focused on the end time cataclysm, which they expected any day. "Speaking generally, the prophets foretold the future that should arise out of the present, while the apocalyptists

11

foretold the future that should break into the present."[4] This is a generaliza-
tion, for even in the prophets we find God breaking into history (Isaiah
63:1-6).

Apocalyptists were dualists. That is, they saw two supernatural powers
in conflict: God and Satan. But unlike their Persian counterparts who
thought the opposites were equal, the Jewish apocalyptists believed that
Satan was created by and subordinate to God. Corresponding to the two
powers were two worlds or ages: the present one, which is temporal, evil, and
under Satan's control; and the coming one, which is timeless, perfect, and
under God's direct rule. To an apocalyptist, there was nothing man or anyone
else could do to fight the evils in this world, nor anything Satan or anyone
else could do to prevent God from ultimately destroying the evil world. History is determined.

The symbols of apocalypses were often fantastic, but a common stock
grew up over the years. Today, political cartoons around the world share certain symbols that readers recognize: the eagle for the United States, the bear
for Russia, the lion for Britain, the dragon for China. In the same way, for
instance, first-century readers recognized the sea monster as representing the
great enemy of God.[5]

A typical apocalypse would claim to be an ancient person's vision of the
history between his time and the end. That history would be portrayed in
vivid pictures abounding in strange creatures. The events would be fairly
recognizable up until the time of the real author (who had simply cast past
history as predictive prophecy), but would become vague thereafter.

Prophecy

We can see how Revelation is like apocalypse. It uses the same kinds of symbols. It promises that God will break into history to bring the new heavens
and earth. There is a cosmic struggle between God and Satan. Many of the
revelations come through angels. But the differences are crucial:

1. Every other known apocalypse is written under the name of some
ancient illustrious person. This lent authority to the book that the author
did not claim to possess. But John writes Revelation under his own name, as
though he has Christ's authority to declare what will be.

2. Along the same lines, the apocalyptists knew they were writing
during a time when the voice of prophecy was silent. But John claims to be
writing prophecy (1:3; 22:7,10,18-19), even "the word of God" (1:2).

3. Fittingly, we find throughout Revelation the prophetic concern for
moral action that is absent in other apocalypses (2:1-3:22, 16:15, 21:8). John
does not share the apocalyptic pessimism that there can be anything good in
the present.

4. While the apocalypses look exclusively to the future for deliverance,
Revelation focuses on a decisive work that has already been accomplished:
the Lamb has already been slain and has already redeemed for Himself a
people (5:6-10). The apocalypses await a future Messiah; John asserts that He
has already come and won His great victory through death and resurrection.

5. John does not retrace past history in the guise of prophecy, but as a true prophet declares what he has really seen of the present and the future.

6. Just as the Old Testament prophets saw real present situations as types of end time ones, so does John. For example, it is often hard to tell whether Isaiah is talking about the redemption of Israel from exile in Babylon or about the redemption of God's people in the last days. The contemporary historical event foreshadows the ultimate event. Likewise, it is often hard to tell whether John is talking about Rome or the ultimate evil empire, since God showed him the ultimate in terms he could understand—for John, Rome embodied the spirit of the ultimate evil empire.

7. The visions in apocalypses are often so strange that the words depend on interpretations by the heavenly guide. This happens in Revelation (17:7-18), but more often John simply leaves the reader to interpret the vision.

Clearly, John's book is both apocalypse and prophecy. The emphasis is not on satisfying idle curiosity (the Revelation raises more speculative questions than it answers) but on motivating people to live a certain way. The blessing in 22:7 is for acting on the prophecy, and one cannot act on a mere forecast. Contrary to what many people believe, the chief feature of prophecy is not foretelling the future (although it may do that) but telling forth God's message (warning, promise, command, encouragement) to believers in their current situations.[6]

Epistle

It is easy to overlook the fact that this prophecy is also a letter from a prominent Church figure to seven churches in the Roman province of Asia. Like all the New Testament epistles, this one is for all Christians in all generations, but there is equally a note of urgency and immediacy in a letter sent to seven particular groups of believers.

This is why we ask when and by whom a letter was written: the more we know about the original circumstances, the better we can grasp what the writer was getting at. The author was a Jewish Christian named John, someone highly respected among the churches of the Roman province of Asia (now part of Turkey). Tradition has it that this was the Apostle John. This tradition has been challenged, but it still seems to be the best conclusion from the evidence.[7]

John was on Patmos, a little island off the coast of Asia, because of the persecution described on pages 9-10. (Patmos held a Roman penal colony; John was either imprisoned there or ministering to those who were.) It was probably the end of the reign of Domitian (about 95 AD) or possibly in the reign of Nero (about 68 AD).[8]

First Impressions

This introduction may have given you more information than you can handle at this point. If so, disregard it. The best way to begin studying a book of the

13

Bible is to read it through to gather your own impressions. Revelation may seem long and confusing, but remember that God has attached both a blessing and an urgency to reading it (1:3). So, try to read the whole book in one or two sittings—not stopping to unravel the details but absorbing the overall flavor. As you read, jot notes under questions 1 through 3.

1. What are your first impressions about John's style of writing? (Does it seem more like a documentary, a theater production, cartoon animation, a logical essay? Is it fun or difficult? Why?) What are your impressions of his tone or mood (optimistic, pessimistic, angry, joyful, fearful, calm, cynical, excited . . .)?

_____

_____

_____

_____

_____

2. Repetition is a clue to the ideas an author wants to emphasize. What words and phrases recur often in Revelation?

_____

_____

_____

_____

_____

3. What questions about the book arise from your first reading? What would you like to find out more about as you study in detail? Also, what questions do you have about the introductory material on pages 9-13?

_____

_____

_____

_____

_____

4. The next step in an overview is to break the book into major sections, then break those sections into parts. This gives you a working outline to see how the book is put together. To save you time, we have suggested some divisions on the following pages. Go back through the book, and make up a title for each major and secondary section. (Feel free to alter the divisions; they are arbitrary in some places.)

If you have trouble making up titles for all of these passages now, do only the main sections and fill in the subsections as you study each lesson.

1:1-20 _____

    1:1-8 _____

    1:9-20 _____

2:1-3:22 _____

    2:1-7 _____

    2:8-11 _____

    2:12-17 _____

    2:18-29 _____

    3:1-6 _____

    3:7-13 _____

    3:14-22 _____

4:1-5:14 _____

    4:1-11 _____

    5:1-14 _____

6:1-8:5 _____

    6:1-17 _____

    7:1-8 _____

    7:9-17 _____

    8:1-5 _____

8:6-11:19 _____

    8:6-9:21 _____

10:1-11 _____

11:1-13 _____

11:14-19 _____

12:1-14:20 _____

12:1-17 _____

13:1-10 _____

13:11-18 _____

14:1-5 _____

14:6-13 _____

14:14-20 _____

15:1-16:21 _____

15:1-8 _____

16:1-21 _____

17:1-19:5 _____

17:1-18 _____

18:1-24 _____

19:1-5 _____

19:6-22:5 _____

19:6-10 _____

19:11-21 _____

20:1-6 _____

20:7-15 _____

21:1-22:5 _____

22:6-21 _____

22:6-11 _____

22:12-17 _____

22:18-21 _____

5. From your first reading of Revelation, what would you say the book is about? What is its major message, or what are its chief themes?

_____

_____

_____

_____

_____

_____

Study Skill—Application

A blessing is offered to those who not only read Revelation but "take to heart what is written in it" (1:3) and "keep" the lessons it teaches (22:7). Therefore, the last step of every study of this book should always be to ask yourself, "What differences should this passage make to my life? How should it make me want to think or act?" Application will require time, thought, prayer, and perhaps even discussion with another person.

At times you may find it most productive to concentrate on one specific application, giving it careful thought and prayer. At other times you may want to list many implications a passage of Scripture has for your life, meditating on them all for several days before you choose one for concentrated prayer and action. Use whatever method helps you take to heart and act on what the passage says.

6. Did your first reading suggest anything that you would like to take to heart and act on during the coming week? If so, what is it, and what do you plan to do about it?

_____

_____

_____

_____

_____

_____

For the group

This "For the group" section and the ones in later lessons are intended to suggest ways of structuring your discussions. Feel free to select what suits your group and ignore the rest. The main goals of this lesson are to get to know Revelation as a whole and the people with whom you are going to study it.

Worship. Some groups like to begin with prayer and/or singing. Some share requests for prayer at the beginning, but leave the actual prayer until after the study. Others prefer just to chat and have refreshments for a while and then move to the study, leaving worship until the end. It is a good idea to start with at least a brief prayer for the Holy Spirit's guidance and some silence to help everyone change focus from the day's busyness to the Scripture.

Revelation contains more hymns and scenes of worship than any other New Testament book. As you go through it, you might plan to choose songs and prayers that reflect the passage being studied. Many of the hymns of Revelation have been set to music countless times over the past two thousand years, and modern folk and hymn arrangements are available.

Warm-up. The beginning of a new study is a good time to lay a foundation for honest sharing of ideas, to get comfortable with each other, and to encourage a sense of common purpose. One way to establish common ground is to talk about what each group member hopes to get out of your group—out of your study of Revelation, and out of any prayer, singing, sharing, outreach, or anything else you might do together. Why do you want to study the Bible, and Revelation in particular? If you have someone write down each member's hopes and expectations, then you can look back at these goals later to see if they are being met. Allow about fifteen minutes for this discussion so that it does not degenerate into vague chatting.

How to use this study. If the group has never used a LIFECHANGE study guide before, you might take a whole meeting to get acquainted, discuss your goals, and go over the "How to Use This Study" section on pages 5-8. Then you can take a second meeting to discuss the overview. This will assure that everyone understands the study and will give you more time to read all of Revelation and answer the overview questions.

Go over the parts of the "How to Use This Study" section that you think the group should especially notice. For example, point out the optional questions in the margins. These are available as group discussion questions, ideas for application, and suggestions for further study. It is unlikely that anyone will have time or desire to answer all the optional questions. A person might do one "Optional Application" for any given lesson. You might choose one or two "For Thought and Discussion" questions for your group discussion, or you might spend all your time on the numbered questions. If someone wants to write answers to the optional questions, suggest that he use a separate notebook. It will also be helpful for discussion notes, prayer requests, answers to prayers, application plans, and so on.

Invite everyone to ask questions about how to use the study guide and how your discussions will go.

Reading. It is often helpful to refresh everyone's memory by reading the passage aloud before discussing the questions. Reading all of Revelation is probably out of the question, but you might ask someone to read chapter 1, using the tones of voice he or she thinks John and Jesus would have used. Try to make the chapter sound like living people talking.

Introduction. Ask some questions to bring out the important points of the background on pages 9-13. Here are some examples:

1. How is your situation like the first-century situation in which John wrote Revelation? How is it different?

2. What seems important to know about apocalyptic writing? In what ways is Revelation like other writings called apocalypses? In what ways is it different?

3. What do you think people need to know about biblical prophecy? (Is it strictly foretelling the future?) What features mark Revelation as a prophecy?

4. Why is it important that Revelation is an epistle (a letter)?

First impressions. The introduction on pages 9-13 gives some elements of John's style that you might want to point out. But question 1 is meant primarily to draw out group members' reactions to this unusual book.

Compare your answers to question 4. You might also look together at some outlines of Revelation in study Bibles or commentaries. Remember that there is no one right way to title a passage.

Question 5—a basic statement of what the book is about—is crucial. The introduction suggests some ideas, and your first reading should offer others.

Give everyone a chance to share questions about the introduction and the book. It is good to clear up any confusion as early as possible. However, don't answer any questions that deal with specific passages. Write those down and let the group answer them when you get to the passages.

If you have time and are reasonably comfortable with one another, you might each tell briefly how you were raised to interpret Revelation. You don't want to start off with an argument, but you might want to know where everyone is "coming from." Somehow, you need to establish an atmosphere where no reasonable interpretation is taboo, where group members are allowed to critique each other's views with humility and kindness, and where outrageous interpretations can be gently neutralized.

We have deliberately said nothing about the millenium, the rapture, or the tribulation. These issues will come up in later lessons, and you'll get a chance to draw your own conclusions.

Application. If application is new to some group members, you might make up some sample applications together. Choose a paragraph or verse and think of how it is relevant to you and some specific things you could each do about it. Share your answers to question 6. If there is real confusion about application, see the Study Skill on page 17.

Wrap-up. The group leader should have read lesson two and its "For the group" section. At this point, he or she might give a short summary of what members can expect in that lesson and the coming meeting. This is a chance to whet everyone's appetite, assign any optional questions, omit any numbered questions, or forewarn members of possible difficulties.

Encourage any members who found the overview especially difficult. Some people are better at seeing the big picture than others. Some are best at analyzing a particular verse or paragraph, while others are strongest at seeing how a passage applies to their lives. Urge members to give thanks for their own and others' strengths, and to give and request help when needed. The group is a place to learn from each other. Later lessons will draw on the gifts of close analyzers as well as overviewers and appliers, practical as well as theoretical thinkers.

Worship. Many groups like to end with singing and/or prayer. This can include songs and prayers that respond to what you've learned in Revelation or prayers for specific needs of group members. Some people are shy about sharing personal needs or praying aloud in groups, especially before they know the other people well. If this is true of your group, then a song and/or some silent prayer, and a short closing prayer spoken by the leader, might be an appropriate end. You could also share requests and pray in pairs.

1. G. R. Beasley-Murray, *The Book of Revelation* (Grand Rapids, Michigan: William B. Eerdmans Publishing Company, 1974), page 38.
2. The material on "apocalyptic" is from Robert H. Mounce, *The Book of Revelation* (Grand Rapids, Michigan: William B. Eerdmans Publishing Company, 1977), pages 18-25; Leon Morris, *The Revelation of St. John* (Grand Rapids, Michigan: William B. Eerdmans Publishing Company, 1969), pages 22-25; Beasley-Murray, pages 14-19.
3. Beasley-Murray, page 14.
4. H. H. Rowley, *The Relevance of Apocalyptic* (New York: Association Press, 1963), page 38, quoted in Mounce, page 20.
5. Some people believe that the dragons and bears in Scripture correspond to China and Russia because of their modern meanings. But over the centuries, dragons, bears, lions, and eagles have represented many nations. The eagle was Rome's emblem, for instance, and the dragon represents Wales. We should be careful about reading our familiar symbols back into a book written 1900 years ago.
6. Gerhard Friedrich, "Prophets," *Theological Dictionary of the New Testament,* volume 6 (Grand Rapids, Michigan: William B. Eerdmans Publishing Company, 1964), pages 849-850; quoted in Beasley-Murray, page 22.
7. Readers interested in the debate about authorship should see the appropriate sections in any of the commentaries listed on pages 163-164. Those will refer you to other sources.
8. See the appropriate sections in the commentaries.

REVELATION 1:1-20

The Son of Man

Imagine yourself as a member of a tiny and embattled church. False and unscrupulous teachers are splitting your congregation. Members of a rival religious group are stirring up trouble for you in your community. Even the government is making it dangerous for you to remain faithful to the Lord. Now a letter arrives from the most respected Christian leader in your area, and you are asked to read it to the assembled church. Read John's introductory words in 1:1-20 aloud with expression and meaning. Listen to yourself as you read, and ask God to let these words have their full impact upon you.

For Thought and Discussion: Do you think the first phrase of 1:1 means "the revelation *from* Jesus," "the revelation *about* Jesus," or both? Why?

Prologue (1:1-3)

Blessed (1:3). The first of seven "beatitudes" or blessings offered in Revelation. (The others are 14:13; 16:15; 19:9; 20:6; 22:7,14.)

1. According to 1:1-3, why did God give this revelation? Also, what responses does He want its hearers to make?

_____

_____

_____

For Further Study:
Watch for sevens in
the rest of Revelation.
Decide for yourself
what symbolism (if
any) you think the
number seven has in
each case.

Greetings and praise (1:4-8)

The customary way to begin a Greek letter was,
"Sender to Recipient, Greetings" (Acts 23:26). John
gives this an explicitly Christian form. Keep in mind
as you study further passages that the whole of
Revelation was originally an urgent letter from a
pastor to his struggling flock.

The seven churches in the province of Asia (1:4).
They are listed in 1:11 and shown on the map
on page 9. There were other churches in Asia
(such as Colosse [Colossians 1:2]; Troas [Acts
20:5]; and Hierapolis [Colossians 4:13]). Why
did John write to just these seven? Since they
lay "on the great circular road that bound
together the most populous, wealthy, and
influential parts of the province,"[1] they may
have been the heads of seven groups into which
the Asian church was organized. Or they may
have been the province's seven postal centers.[2]
Or these seven may have been John's special
responsibility.
    The number *seven* recurs fifty-two[3] times
in Revelation. Because of its association with
the Sabbath and the seven days of creation, this
number signifies completeness, perfection, and
the essence of a thing. The universe revolves in
a seven-day week; Old Testament sacrifices were
done in sevens; *seven* is the root of the Hebrew
word for swearing an oath.[4] So, the seven individual, historical churches of Asia may represent
for John the complete church of Asia or the
complete Church of all generations that needs
to hear this message.
    It may be that all of these explanations
are true.

Grace and peace (1:4). Like Paul (1 Corinthians
1:1-3), John replaces the "greetings" in his
letter with an explicitly Christian "Grace and

22

peace to you." "Grace" refers to God's presence with the believer that empowers him to live the Christian life. "Peace" summarizes the blessings that flow from God's presence.

Him who is, and who was, and who is to come (1:4). "An adaptation of the name of God made known to Moses at the bush, Exodus 3:14." The Greek translation of the Old Testament rendered this name as "I am who I am" and "I am he who is." One of the commentary paraphrases that circulated among Jewish congregations expanded this to "I am he who is and who will be." In Deuteronomy 32:39, this paraphrase reads, "I am he who is, and who was, and I am he who will be."[5] Thus, John is building on a familiar title for God.

Optional Application: What difference does it make to you that God is He "who is to come"? How should this affect the way you deal with your circumstances and the people around you?

2. The Jews were used to calling God "him who was, and who is, and who will be." John changed this to "him who is, and who was, and who *is to come*" (1:4). What might be his point(s) in doing this? (Consider 2:16; 3:11; 22:7,12,20.)

_____

_____

_____

_____

_____

Seven spirits before his throne (1:4). Since seven signifies perfection and essence, most interpreters think the seven spirits "represent the Holy Spirit in his fullness of life and blessing."[6] Thus, 1:4-5 is a blessing from each member of the Trinity.

Before the main body of his letter, John inserts a hymn of praise to Jesus (1:5-6) and a short prophecy

For Thought and Discussion: To what truths is Jesus a faithful witness (1:5)?

For Thought and Discussion: How has Jesus "freed us from our sins by his blood" (Revelation 1:5)? See Romans 3:21-26 and Hebrews 9:11-10:18.

(1:7-8). Even before the vision of 1:12-20, we have a striking portrait of Christ.

3. What does it mean that Jesus is "the firstborn from the dead" (1:5)? How did He become the firstborn? (*Optional:* See 1 Corinthians 15:3-4,20-28.)

_____

_____

_____

_____

_____

4. How is it personally important to you that Jesus . . .

is "the faithful witness" (1:5)?

_____

_____

_____

_____

_____

is "the firstborn from the dead" (1:5)?

_____

_____

_____

_____

_____

is "the ruler of the kings of the earth" (1:5)?

_____

_____

_____

_____

_____

"loves us and has freed us from our sins by his blood" (1:5)?

_____

_____

_____

_____

_____

5. What does it imply about you that Jesus "has made us to be a kingdom and priests to serve his God and Father" (1:6)?

kingdom (see, for example, 2:26-27, 5:10)

_____

_____

_____

_____

priests (Romans 12:1; Hebrews 10:19-22; 1 Peter 2:5,9)

_____

_____

_____

_____

_____

The Alpha and the Omega (1:8). Alpha is the first letter of the Greek alphabet, and omega is the last. Compare 1:17.

Optional Application: Thank Jesus for one or more of the truths about Him in question 4. How should you act in light of it? (For example, how should you act now that you are freed from sin by His blood?)

Optional Application: How can you act as a priest to serve the Father this week?

For Further Study:
Watch for what John
has to say about "the
suffering and king-
dom and patient
endurance that are
ours in Jesus" (1:9) in
the rest of the book.

For Further Study:
To understand the
meaning of the lamp-
stands better, see
Zechariah 4:1-6 and
Matthew 5:14-15.

The vision (1:9-20)

Suffering (1:9). "Tribulation" in KJV. Evidently,
John felt that he and his readers were already
suffering a "tribulation" in their day. This is
just what Jesus promised (John 16:33). However, it leaves open the question of whether
Revelation teaches that there will be a last,
ultimate tribulation just before the Lord's
return.

Likewise, the *kingdom* already belonged
to John and his readers *in Jesus*. The Kingdom
of God arrived when Jesus came the first time
(Luke 17:21), and His death and resurrection
already made His people "a kingdom and
priests" (Revelation 1:6). Yet this does not
negate the fact that the Kingdom will not be
consummated until Christ's return (2:26-27).

It is the common teaching of the New Testament that the "last days" began at Jesus' first
coming (Acts 2:14-21) and will be fulfilled at
His second.

---

6. When "a voice like a trumpet" commands John
to "Write . . . what you see," John turns to see
the voice (1:10-12). What John sees recalls
visions that the prophet Daniel had centuries
earlier. What do the following passages help you
understand about John's vision in Revelation
1:12-16?

Daniel 7:9-10 _____

_____

_____

_____

_____

Daniel 7:13-14 _____

_____

_____

26

Daniel 10:4-6 _____

_____

_____

_____

_____

For Further Study:
Using a concordance
(see page 165),
research the Old Tes-
tament symbolism of:
   a. fire (What do
"eyes like blazing
fire" signify?)
   b. bronze (Brass
in KJV. What do feet
like white-hot bronze
represent?)

7. What does the "sharp double-edged sword"
(1:16) seem to signify? (Consider Isaiah 49:2;
Hebrews 4:12; Revelation 2:16; 19:15,21.)

_____

_____

_____

_____

**For Thought and
Discussion:** What
does it mean that
Jesus holds the seven
stars in His hand
(1:16,20)? Why is
this important to you?

8. Why do you think John "fell at his feet as
though dead" (1:17) when he saw this Person?

_____

_____

_____

_____

_____

Hades (1:18). The abode of the dead.

9. a. What truths about Himself does Christ emphasize in 1:17-18?

_____

_____

_____

_____

27

For Further Study:
Find twenty-four titles
for Christ in 1:1-20.
Then look for each
one repeated else-
where in the book.
What does each title
tell you about Jesus?

b. Why are these so important? How are they
relevant to your life, and how should they
affect your attitudes and actions?

_____

_____

_____

_____

_____

10. What overall impression does 1:10-18 give you
of Christ?

_____

_____

_____

_____

***What you have seen, what is now and what will
take place later*** (1:19). Many people take this
verse as a clue to the structure of the book.
There are two main views among those who
think this:
　　1. A three-fold division. "What you have
seen" is the vision of 1:12-18. "What is now" is
the letters to the seven churches of John's time
(2:1-3:22). "What will take place later" is everything from 4:1 on.
　　2. A two-fold division. "What you have
seen" is parallel to "what you see" (1:11); it
encompasses both "what is now" and "what will
take place later." (The Greek of "what you have
seen" allows this interpretation.) The sense is:
"Write, therefore, the things you are about to
see, that is, both what now is and what lies in
the future."[7] Many of those who hold this view
do not try to outline the book on the basis of this
verse. They say that there is a mixture of "now"
and "later" throughout the book, or that chapters 4 through 19 describe the spiritual battle
that has gone on throughout Christian history.

Mystery (1:20). Not a puzzle to be unraveled in the modern sense of a mystery. In the Bible, a mystery is something that humans could never work out for themselves but that God has now revealed.[8] Thus a mystery is not a secret still hidden, but a secret now revealed.

The Lord regards Revelation as the unveiling of a mystery, not a puzzle set for us to solve. Ironically, when He explains a mystery by saying stars=angels of churches, many modern readers feel He is setting an even harder puzzle, not disclosing a secret.

Your response

11. What one truth from 1:1-20 stands out as something you would like to take to heart this week?

_____

_____

_____

_____

_____

12. Why is this truth especially important to you?

_____

_____

_____

_____

13. How would you like this truth to affect the way you act and think—your character and habits?

_____

_____

_____

14. What steps can you take to begin making this happen, by God's grace?

_____

_____

_____

_____

_____

15. List any questions you have about 1:1-20.

_____

_____

_____

_____

_____

For the group

Worship.

Warm-up. People often come to Bible studies with their minds still churning over the day's events. Singing and prayer can help people refocus onto God and His Word. Another method you may find helpful is to begin with a question that deals with people's lives and is related to the topic at hand.

For example, whether we realize it or not, most of us have some mental picture of Jesus. Ask a few people to describe how they imagine Jesus (such as a serene young man in a sort of bathrobe, smiling at you). This is not meant to encourage an idolatry of one's own image of Jesus, but rather the reverse: to help each of you recognize how you do see Jesus, and how your view compares with the way Jesus appeared to John. After you discuss 1:1-20, compare your mental pictures to John's vision.

Read aloud. Ask someone to read 1:1-20 aloud with the tone of voice he or she thinks is appropriate.

Summarize. Basically, what is chapter 1 about?

Questions. You may sometimes need to ask questions that lie behind the numbered questions. For instance, before question 4, ask what it means to be a faithful witness, freed from sins, and so on—just as in question 3. Or, before question 6, ask what John sees.

Feel free to discuss only some of the questions. Be sure to save at least ten or fifteen minutes to discuss how 1:1-20 applies to each of you, and what you plan to do about it. Use the "Optional Applications" as suggestions.

In situations like question 2, this study guide tends to say "John wrote" instead of "the Holy Spirit wrote." Both are equally true, of course, and the terminology is not meant to deny that the Spirit both gave the visions and guided John's recording of them. Feel free to reword questions for your discussion if your group prefers to do so.

Your group might find it fun to draw pictures of what John sees in 1:12-20 (you could also do this with later visions in the book). Some of John's visions are more like animated movies than paintings, but it might be enlightening to compare how different group members visualize what John describes.

Summarize. Summarize your discussion: what the chapter says, and how it applies to you.

Wrap-up.

Worship. Use 1:4-8,12-18 as springboards for your own praise of the Father, the Spirit, and especially the Son. Praise Them for the attributes John mentions.

Four Views

Since the writing of the book of Revelation, there have been four main schools of thought on how to interpret it:[9]

1. *Preterists* understand the book almost exclusively in terms of the first century. They believe John is talking only about the Roman Empire and the early Church, and that almost all of the events in the book were fulfilled either at the fall of Jerusalem (70 AD) or the fall of Rome (476 AD). This is the view of many modern schol-

(continued on page 32)

(continued from page 31)
ars outside conservative evangelicalism.

2. *Historicists* take the book as a forecast of the course of history up to their own time. "Of little significance to its initial readers, the Apocalypse was held to sketch the history of western Europe through the various popes, the Protestant Reformation, the French Revolution, and individual leaders such as Charlemagne and Mussolini."[10] Historicists have varied widely in the people and events they have identified with each of John's visions, and they have tended to assume that their own time is the last.

3. *Futurists* think that from chapter 4 on, Revelation is about what will happen at the end of the world—the events that will usher in the Second Coming of Christ and the final victory of God over the forces of evil. A strict futurist would say that Revelation has nothing to do with what will happen until the last few years before the Second Coming. Among futurists, some think the visions in Revelation are in chronological order, others think the three sets of seven judgments (seals, trumpets, bowls) are in chronological order but the other visions are not, and still others think the seals, trumpets, and bowls look at the same timespan from different angles.

4. *Idealists* believe that Revelation is not talking about specific events at all, whether past, present, or future. Rather, it portrays poetic pictures of timeless ideas and principles, such as the triumph of good over evil and how God acts in history.

1. W. M. Ramsay, *The Letters to the Seven Churches of Asia* (Grand Rapids, Michigan: Baker Book House, 1963 [1904]), page 183.
2. *The NIV Study Bible*, edited by Kenneth Barker (Grand Rapids, Michigan: Zondervan Corporation, 1985), page 1926.
3. *The NIV Study Bible*, page 1923.
4. Michael Wilcock, *I Saw Heaven Opened* (Downers Grove, Illinois: InterVarsity Press, 1975), page 62.
5. Beasley-Murray, page 54, citing the Jerusalem Targum.
6. Beasley-Murray, page 56.
7. Mounce, pages 41-43; Morris, page 56.
8. Morris, page 56.
9. Mounce, pages 16-18.
10. Mounce, page 42.

REVELATION 2:1-3:22

The Seven Churches

Have you ever noticed that in the New Testament, God speaks to His people through personal letters more than in any other way? Perhaps this reflects His desire for intimate relationship. Whether the Lord has happy words to say or harsh ones, at least the recipient of His letters knows he has the Lord's attention.

Some people think the letters in 2:1-3:22 are purely a literary device, that the messages are really directed to every church and individual believer in every generation. Others, noting how appropriate each message is to the particular church, think Jesus really was addressing seven specific congregations. Most interpreters feel that as with the other New Testament epistles, we should keep both of these perspectives in mind. In addition, some people believe that the seven churches also speak prophetically of seven ages of Church history. (See pages 49-50.)

Read 2:1-3:22, preferably aloud. Ask God to open your ears to hear what the Spirit is saying to you. As you read, observe how each letter follows and deviates from this basic pattern:

    a. Address.
    b. One or two titles of Jesus (often from 1:13-18).
    c. Commendation.
    d. Criticism.
    e. Counsel.
    f. Command: "He who has ears. . . ."
    g. Promise to overcomers.

For Thought and Discussion: Consider the repeated refrain that ends (or almost ends) Jesus' word to each church (such as 2:29). Does this suggest that these prophetic words are meant only for the specific church addressed, or for others? Why? Does this refrain prove that the words are not for specific churches? Why or why not?

For Further Study:
a. To learn more about Ephesus, read Acts 18:18-20:38 and Paul's letter to the Ephesians.
b. Compare Paul's words in Acts 20:29-31 (about 57 AD) to Revelation 2:2-3 (about 98 AD). What do you observe?

Optional Application: Are you holding fast to your first love? How do your actions show or not show it? Pray about this, and take steps if necessary.

For Thought and Discussion: a. What do you think "I will come to you and remove your lampstand" (2:5) means?

b. Here Jesus warns "I will come" not just on some distant date, but soon. What are the implications for your life now?

Ephesus (2:1-7)

Over a quarter of a million people lived in Ephesus,[1] the chief seaport of Asia and one of the foremost cities of the Empire. Through Ephesus passed goods from China and the eastern provinces bound for Italy. Wide avenues, huge public buildings and squares, and luxurious private homes were designed to impress tourists. The theater could hold twenty-five thousand people. Ephesus flaunted dozens of temples for various gods, but it was world famous for the one dedicated to Ephesian Artemis, a mother-goddess. Gold, marble, and jewels adorned this 425-foot long structure. The citizens also prided themselves that Ephesus was the warden of two temples dedicated to the worship of the emperor.[2] Further, the city was known for magical scrolls called "Ephesian letters."[3]

By the end of the first century, the church in Ephesus was probably the largest and most influential one in the world. The Apostle Paul and his colleagues established it in about 52-55 BC (Acts 19), and he later sent his protege Timothy to pastor the church there (1 Timothy 1:3). Tradition has it that John himself lived there before and after he wrote Revelation.

The name *Ephesus* means "maiden of choice" or "desirable."[4]

1. The rebuke Jesus has for the Ephesian church is "You have forsaken your first love" (2:4). What do you think this means? (*Optional:* See Jeremiah 2:2, Matthew 22:37-38.)

_____

_____

_____

_____

2. Why is this so serious that it merits the threat of removal of the lampstand (2:5)?

_____

_____

For Further Study:
To understand "the right to eat from the tree of life" (Revelation 2:7), study Genesis 2:8-9,15-17; 3:22-24; and Revelation 22:1-2. What is the tree of life? What is the paradise of God?

Apostles (2:2). As a center of trade and tourism, Ephesus received more than its share of traveling teachers who claimed to know the way to bliss and wisdom. They often collected ideas from many philosophies and religions—the more esoteric, the better. The New Testament is full of references to such itinerants who mixed a little Christianity into their doctrines to make them palatable in churches.

Nicolaitans (2:6,15). These may or may not be the same as the false apostles. According to second-century tradition, the Nicolaitans believed in a heavenly Christ but downgraded the earthly Jesus as a mere man. They also emphasized the immediate inspiration of the Holy Spirit over the apostolic teachings of Paul, Peter, and John. They held a belief, popular at the time, that matter is evil and only spirit is good. Some who believed this became rigid ascetics, but the Nicolaitans apparently decided that anything one did with one's body was acceptable as long as one's spirit was united with God. This meant that a Christian was free to do immoral acts. Second-century sources say the Nicolaitans shared all their goods, including their wives.[5]

    An alternate understanding is that *Nicolaitan* comes from *nikeo* (to overcome, to conquer) and *laos* (the people, the laity). Some interpreters think Jesus nicknamed "Nicolaitans" those who promoted the idea of the clergy or hierarchy ruling over the people instead of being shepherds who served the people.

Remove your lampstand (2:5). The lampstand is the church in this city. By the sixth century AD, Ephesus was deserted. The harbor, which was its livelihood, had begun to fill with silt even in John's day, and today the ruins of ancient Ephesus are miles inland.

3. In the chart on page 44, summarize in your own words the strengths and weaknesses of the Ephesian church.

For Further Study:
The seven letters to
the churches in Reve-
lation 2:1-3:22 have
much in common with
prophetic oracles
directed to nations
and individuals in the
Old Testament. Com-
pare them to what the
Lord says to eight
nations in Amos
1:3-2:16. What is
similar and different
about the patterns,
the contents, the
tones of voice? What
do you learn about
prophecy from each
passage?

For Further Study:
On "the second
death" (2:11), see
20:6,14; 21:8.

**For Thought and
Discussion:** Jesus
talks about life and
death over and over to
the Smyrnans. Why do
you think He does
this?

Smyrna (2:8-11)

Although smaller than Ephesus, Smyrna was still
prosperous because it sat on the coast at the end of
a major trade route to the east. Unlike Ephesus, it
continues to be a thriving city to this day—the
second largest in Asiatic Turkey.[6] In John's time it
had been solidly loyal to Rome for centuries and
contained a temple to the goddess of Rome and
another to the emperor.[7] It also boasted a stadium, a
library, and the largest public theater in Asia.[8]

The real danger to Smyrnan Christians was not
the Roman patriots but the large population of Jews
who detested Christians as heretics and inflamed
the Romans to persecute them. One of the most
famous martyrs of the second century was Polycarp,
the bishop of Smyrna. The contemporary record of
his death states that he was "the twelfth to meet a
martyr's death in Smyrna."[9] Polycarp was burned to
death on a Saturday in 155 AD, and the Jews of
Smyrna broke the Sabbath to gather wood for the
fire. They abhorred the ideas that a man executed
for blasphemy was the Messiah and that a person
became pleasing to God not by obeying the Law of
Moses but by putting faith in this Messiah.

Smyrna means "bitter" or "myrrh," a tree resin
with a bitter taste that was crushed and used in per-
fume, in incense, and as a preservative in burial.

4. Jesus begins each letter with a title of Himself
   that is relevant to the theme of the letter. Why
   might 2:8 have been an especially relevant
   reminder for the Smyrnan Christians?

   _____

   _____

   _____

   _____

Crown (2:10). This is not the word for a royal crown
used in 12:3. It can mean the garland or wreath
given to victorious athletes, or the crown of light
that people believed blessed mortals received
when they died.[10] The crown is eternal *life*.

5. On page 44, summarize the character of the church in Smyrna.

Pergamum (2:12-17)

Pergamum was the political capital of Asia, even though Ephesus was larger. It was the center of the imperial cult in the province. In addition to its temple to Caesar and Rome, Pergamum's most popular tourist attraction was the temple of Asclepios, the god of healing. People flocked to the shrine in hopes of miraculous cures. (The myth of Asclepios had its roots in Babylon. His symbol was the serpent; doctors use it today.) Three other major temples also loomed over Pergamum atop its mountain citadel. In particular, "an enormous altar of Zeus . . . stood on a platform on the hill overlooking the city."[11]

The governor of Asia, who resided in Pergamum, was the official champion of both justice and the imperial cult. He held the *ius gladii*, the "right of the sword" to execute anyone he willed (compare 2:12,16).[12]

Pergamum means something like "additional marriage." (*Per* is "elevation" and *gamum* is "marriage.")[13]

Balaam (2:14). King Balak of Moab hired the pagan prophet Balaam to curse Israel. The Lord hindered Balaam from doing this. So, Balaam suggested another route to Israel's downfall. He advised the Midianite women to seduce the Israelite men into idolatry and fornication (Numbers 25:1-2, 31:16).

Sexual immorality (2:14). Literal and spiritual fornication are linked repeatedly in the Bible. Israel is portrayed as the virgin bride of the Lord (Isaiah 54:5, Hosea 2:19) and to consort with other gods is to commit adultery against Him (Jeremiah 13:27, Hosea 2:13). Even pagan nations are called prostitutes because of idolatry (Isaiah 23:16-17, Nahum 3:4). The link between idolatry and fornication was close because the pagan gods were primarily fertility gods and were worshiped with phallic symbols and ritual sex acts.

For Thought and Discussion: Why do you think Jesus emphasizes to Pergamum that He "has the sharp, double-edged sword" (2:12)? Compare 1:16; 2:16; 19:15,21. What is this sword, and what does Jesus use it for? How is it appropriate for Pergamum?

For Thought and Discussion: What do you think Jesus means by calling Pergamum the place "where Satan has his throne" (2:13)?

For Thought and Discussion: What significance might there be that the Lord gives Antipas His own title ("faithful witness"; compare 1:5) in 2:13?

For Further Study:
For more on the hidden manna, see Exodus 16:1-36, Numbers 11:7-9, John 6:48-58.

Optional Application: a. Have you been enticed to commit spiritual adultery, as Balaam enticed Israel?
b. Are you under pressure to put the secular society or government before God in any areas, as Christians were pressured to participate in the emperor's cult?
c. If either of these sounds like your situation, what should you do?

For Further Study:
Read what Paul wrote to Christians in Corinth struggling with whether to attend dinners that included meat sacrificed to a patron god (1 Corinthians 8:1-11:1).

The concepts of the Bride and idolatry= adultery turn up often in Revelation (17:1-5, 19:7-9). We also notice it in the names of Ephesus (the maiden of choice who forsook her first love) and Pergamum (who took a second marriage by consorting with other gods).

Hidden manna (2:17). In contrast to the food of idol worship (2:14), the overcomers will eat the heavenly food, foreshadowed by the manna Israel ate in the wilderness (in Balaam's day).

White stone (2:17). Stones were given in ancient times for many reasons. Three possibilities are:
1. At the end of a trial, the jurors would give the accused a white stone if he was innocent, and a black one if guilty.
2. A stone could be the admission ticket to a festival or assembly.
3. The stone bears the name of Christ or God, a symbol of the power placed in the hands of one who overcomes temptation even to the point of death.[14]

New name (2:17). Either the name of the victor declared innocent and admitted to the Kingdom, or the name of Christ or God that gives him power and authority in the Kingdom. In the ancient world, a name signified a person's character and authority.

6. On page 44, summarize the praiseworthy and blameworthy traits of the Pergamene church.

7. Why do you think the whole Pergamene church needs to repent even though only some of its members follow the corrupt teachings (2:16)?

_____

_____

_____

Thyatira (2:18-29)

Thyatira was not a remarkable city; it was simply a thriving center of manufacturing and marketing.

Practically everyone in town belonged to one of the dozens of trade and craft guilds. Membership in these was crucial, since they were the focus of business and social life. But each was dedicated to a patron god, and meetings included a common meal in its honor. The meat for the meal came from an animal sacrificed to the god. In addition, drunkenness, carousing, and even orgies were not rare. What should a Christian do? Evidently, many in Thyatira who were otherwise full of love and faith were willing to listen to a woman teaching that it was okay to tolerate—even participate in—pagan practices (2:20).[15]

Thyatira means "unweary sacrifice."[16]

Jezebel (2:20). When this pagan princess became queen of Israel, she encouraged Israel to practice idolatry and immorality, including the sexual rites of the fertility deities (1 Kings 16:31; 2 Kings 9:22,30-37). Thus, her name is a fitting nickname for the false prophetess of Thyatira. If she resembled heretics later called *Gnostics*, she was teaching that people in whom the Spirit dwelt did not need to worry about morality, and that they could participate in pagan rites because the pagan gods did not exist.

Commit adultery (2:22). Perhaps both literal and spiritual adultery were involved in the prophetess's pagan teachings.

Her children (2:23). Probably her spiritual children among the members of the church.

Satan's so-called deep secrets (2:24). The word *Gnostic* comes from the Greek word *gnosis* ("knowledge"), for the Gnostics taught that salvation required simply that one know the deep secrets about God and reality. The saved were then free in the Spirit to explore both good and evil and to practice any indulgence of the body. Some Gnostics even "boasted that it was precisely by entering the stronghold of Satan that believers could learn the limits of his power and emerge victorious." The prophetess may have encouraged Christians to participate in pagan rites and orgies to prove that evil could not alter their salvation by grace nor their life in the Spirit.[17]

For Thought and Discussion: a. What do Jesus' "eyes . . . like blazing fire" (2:18) have to do with Thyatira? Consider 2:23.

b. How are His "feet . . . like burnished bronze" (2:18) relevant?

Optional Application: Do you ever run into moral conflicts in your business or social life, as the Christians in Thyatira did? Search out some New Testament principles for handling such situations.

Optional Application: The Ephesian church was strong on resisting false doctrine and immorality but weak on love (2:2-4). The Thyatiran church was strong on love but weak on resisting false doctrine and immorality (2:19-20). Which of these, if either, are you more like? What can you do about this?

For Thought and Discussion: Why is it significant that Revelation 2:27 ascribes to overcomers what Psalm 2:9 ascribes to Christ? (See Romans 8:17.)

For Thought and Discussion: How can a church appear to be alive and thriving, but be dead?

For Thought and Discussion: a. Does Jesus have anything good to say about Sardis, other than the church's reputation? What does that tell you?

b. Jesus gives Sardis no promise of glory and authority, only the assurance that overcomers will not be blotted out from the book of life (3:5). What does this say about the way Jesus views churches like Sardis?

8. On page 45, summarize the good and bad aspects of the Thyatiran church's character.

9. What can we learn about Christ's methods of dealing with His people from 2:21-28?

_____

_____

_____

Sardis (3:1-6)

Sardis had been a rich and glorious city in the fifth and sixth centuries BC. After an earthquake in 17 AD Rome rebuilt Sardis, but the reversal of decay was only temporary. The contrast between past splendor and present decay was notable, although the city was still wealthy. Further, although Sardis was built on a mountain and had a virtually impregnable citadel on a spur of the mountain, it had twice been taken because of unvigilant guards. Sardis was also the commercial center for woolens and was known for its dyeing works. The patron of Sardis was Cybele, an Asian mother-goddess who was said to have the power to restore life to the dead.[18]
Sardis may mean "remnant."[19]

_____

Reputation (3:1). Literally, "name." ***People*** in 3:4 is also "names." See also 3:5.

The book of life (3:5). The register of all the citizens of the Kingdom.

_____

10. How do Christ's words to the church at Sardis reflect the character of the city as a whole, as described above?

_____

_____

_____

_____

11. Summarize the Sardan church's condition on page 45.

12. The church at Sardis was untroubled by persecution from pagans. How was the lack of persecution related to Sardis' problem?

_____

_____

_____

_____

For Thought and Discussion: What is the significance of the white clothes in 3:4-5? (See 6:11; 7:9,13.)

For Thought and Discussion: What is Jesus' point in repeating "name" four times in 3:1-6?

Philadelphia (3:7-13)

Philadelphia was a prosperous little commercial center. Its one main drawback was that it was subject to earthquakes. In fact, after the quake of 17 AD, many of its inhabitants were too nervous to return to the city and settled in the surrounding countryside. For the little church in Philadelphia, the source of instability was the local synagogue, where the Jews may have taunted the Gentile Christians, saying they had no right of access or belonging to the Kingdom of God. In addition, commercial discrimination and even outright mob violence were possibilities.[20]

Philadelphia means "brotherly love."[21]

Key of David (3:7). In Isaiah 22:22, the key of authority over Jerusalem (the city of David) is taken from the worthless steward Shebna and given to the righteous Eliakim. Likewise, the Father has given authority over His Kingdom to Jesus. He may (and does) admit His followers to the Kingdom and exclude His opponents.

Keep you from the hour of trial (3:10). Interpreters generally agree that this trial ("tribulation" KJV) is the one described in chapters 6-19. The letter to Smyrna refers to a trial to test the church—this the believers must undergo (2:10). Now Jesus tells the Philadelphian church it will be kept *from* the trial that will test the world.

41

For Further Study:
What does it mean to
be a true Jew (3:9)?
See Romans 2:2-29.

For Further Study:
Read about the temple pillars in 1 Kings 7:15-22.

Preterists say the tribulation is the persecution Christians endured between 95 and 325 AD. Idealists say it is the whole struggle with the world and Satan between Christ's first and second comings. Futurists say it is a Great Tribulation of the last seven (or three and a half) years of history.

Many futurists see 3:10 as a promise to the faithful Church of the last days. They debate whether it foretells that God will keep the Church from the Great Tribulation by removing them from the earth or by protecting them in the midst of the trouble. The Greek grammar is inconclusive on this point.

Those who live on the earth (3:10). This phrase recurs seven times (6:10; 8:13; 11:10; 13:8,14; 17:8). It refers to mankind hostile to God. These are those who are natives or citizens of this world and identify with it. They are in contrast with those who reside on earth as strangers, as citizens and ambassadors of another Kingdom (2 Corinthians 5:20; Philippians 3:20; Hebrews 11:13-16, 13:14; 1 Peter 1:1).

Pillar (3:12). This symbol of permanence and stability would have encouraged citizens of a town prone to earthquakes. Although 21:22 says there will be no temple in the Holy City, Jesus is not being inconsistent. He is simply using the fluid imagery of apocalyptic. The overcomers are not going to be literal pillars in a literal temple.

Name (3:12). Names express character. "Christ's new name symbolizes all that he is by virtue of his redemptive work for mankind."[22] To write one's name on something denotes ownership and belonging.

13. What encouragements does Jesus offer in 3:7-13 to those suffering persecution?

_____

_____

_____

14. Describe the Philadelphian church's character on page 45.

Laodicea (3:14-22)

Laodicea was a commercial and administrative center, the richest city in its district. In fact, when it was destroyed by an earthquake in 60 AD, Laodicea refused imperial aid that its neighbors gladly accepted. Laodicea "was known throughout the Roman world of its time for three things: its banks, which even Cicero recommended for exchanging money; its linen and wool industry, which produced cloth and carpets, especially from the glossy black wool of sheep reared in the area; its medical school and widely famed medicines, notable among which was an eye-ointment"[23] (see 3:17-18). Laodicea's sister cities were Hierapolis and Colosse. Because Laodicea was built to suit the trade routes rather than natural resources, the city had no local water supply. Water had to be piped through stone conduits. This made the city extremely vulnerable to attack, so its politicians specialized in appeasement.[24] Laodicea had a large Jewish population—at least 7,500 adult males.[25]

Laodicea means "rule of the people" or "judgment of the people."

Lukewarm (3:16). Six miles in one direction, Hierapolis had hot mineral springs useful for medicinal baths. Six miles in another direction, the springs of Denizli were icy cold to refresh thirst. But by the time the water of Hierapolis had flowed across the plateau to the cliffs across from Laodicea, it had lost its heat, was useless for healing, and was merely poisonous to drink. Likewise, by the time the spring water had traveled six miles, it was lukewarm and far less refreshing.[26]

Spit you out of my mouth (3:16). When the mineral water from Hierapolis lost its heat, it spewed lime down the cliff opposite Laodicea—a perpetual reminder of lukewarm, poisonous water spit out of the mouth.[27]

For Thought and Discussion: What is wrong with "rule of the people" in a church? Who should rule?

For Thought and Discussion: In context, is 3:20 addressed to believers or unbelievers? What is the meaning of the verse, in your own words?

Optional Application: Are you hot enough to heal the sick or cold enough to refresh the thirsty? What do your actions testify? Pray about this.

15. In a sense, the seven churches embody the seven conditions in which an individual or a church may find itself at any given time. We usually have traits of several of the churches simultaneously, but they are a good checklist. In your own words, summarize the character of each of the seven churches.

	strengths	weaknesses
Ephesus		
Smyrna		
Pergamum		

	strengths	weaknesses
Thyatira		
Sardis		
Philadelphia		
Laodicea		

Optional Application: Do you act as though you think you are rich or poor in your own resources? Do you need gold, white clothes, and eye-salve from Jesus? Pray about this.

For Thought and Discussion: What does it imply that Jesus describes Himself as *outside the door* from the Christians at Laodicea?

For Thought and Discussion: a. In each letter, Jesus closes (before or after the promise to the overcomers) with the same summons for those with ears to hear. What is the point of this call? Whom do you think He is addressing?

b. Is it significant that Jesus said the same thing when He told parables? What was His point there (Matthew 13:9-17)?

16. What was the Laodicean church's problem? Explain in your own words on page 45.

17. What can we learn about the Lord's character from what He says to the Laodicean church?

_____

_____

_____

_____

18. In 1:9, John calls himself "your brother and companion in the suffering and kingdom and patient endurance that are ours in Jesus."

a. What does Jesus say to the seven churches about suffering? (What did the churches have to suffer, and why? How did Jesus want them to respond, and why?)

2:2-3 _____

_____

_____

2:9-10 _____

_____

_____

2:13 _____

_____

_____

2:22-23 _____

_____

_____

3:10 _____

_____

_____

46

b. What do you learn about the Kingdom from the seven letters? (See especially 2:7,11,17,26-28; 3:3-5,11-12,14,20-21.)

_____

_____

_____

_____

_____

c. What does Jesus say about patient endurance (2:2-3,7,10-11,13,17,19,25-26; 3:4-5,8-12,21)?

_____

_____

_____

_____

19. Look back at the chart in question 15. What if Jesus came to you personally with a message like the seven? What would He say to you about each of the following?

"I know where you live" (2:13) _____

_____

_____

_____

"I know your deeds" (2:2,19; 3:1,8,15) _____

_____

_____

_____

_____

_____

_____

For Further Study:
a. Compare the title Jesus gives Himself in each message (such as in 2:1) to the rest of the message. How is each title appropriate?
b. Do the same with the promise to overcomers in each message.
c. How do the titles and promises help you grasp what Jesus is saying to each church?

Optional Application: Apply question 19 to your church or fellowship as a group.

Optional Application: Which of the seven churches are you most like? What should you do about this?

Optional Application: How can you go about acquiring one or more of the traits Jesus commends, such as love, faith, resistance to false teaching, perseverance under persecution, and noncompromise with pagan practices?

For Thought and Discussion: How would you summarize Jesus' message to the seven churches?

Your response

20. What action would you like to take in light of what you have just said about yourself? Consider Jesus' counsel to each church (2:5,10,16,25; 3:2-3,11,18-20).

_____

_____

_____

_____

_____

21. List any questions you have about 2:1-3:22.

_____

_____

_____

For the group

Warm-up. Take a few minutes to share how 1:1-20 affected your lives. How did your efforts at application go? What did you learn about yourselves? What did you find hard or beneficial about focusing on a particular issue for application? This is not a time to impress or embarrass each other, but a time to learn from and about each other.

Read aloud. You might have a different person read each letter.

Summarize. Ask someone to tell what 2:1-3:22 is basically about.

Questions. You may find it difficult to discuss all the questions in equal detail in one meeting. Plan either to select just some of the questions or to take two meetings for this lesson. Be sure to allow enough time to share your answers to question 19. Since this will be partly confession, agree together not to repeat anything that is said. If you haven't developed enough trust to reveal your answers fully, give group members permission to share only as deeply as they feel comfortable. However, if you do detect reluctance to be open, plan to look for ways to overcome it and build trust. What are the obstacles to intimacy in your group?

You might try applying question 19 to your group as a whole. What do you think Jesus would say in a letter to your group?

Commit yourselves to praying for each other during the week regarding each person's desires for application. One of the main reasons for sharing applications as a group is to support each other in prayer.

Summarize. Ask one or two people to summarize Jesus' message to the churches.

Worship. Praise Jesus for holding the stars of the churches in His hands, for walking in the midst of the lampstands-churches, for being the First and the Last, and so on. Thank Him for all the promises He has made to those who overcome temptation and persecution. Ask Him to enable you to obey His commands.

Seven Ages of the Church

Some people believe the seven letters not only describe seven first-century churches but also prophesy the history of the Church from John's time onward.[28] This analysis does reflect a partisan view of history, but we offer it for you to evaluate.

1. *Ephesus* represents the apostolic Church, about 30-100 AD. It grew cooler in its love for the Lord as it grew stronger in doctrinal purity.

2. *Smyrna* is the persecuted Church, a maligned minority between 100 and 313 AD.

3. *Pergamum* is the Church married to or compromising with the state. Emperor Constantine declared Christianity to be the state religion in 313 AD. From then on, the emperors had a strong say in what the Church did, and pagan practices were Christianized.

4. *Thyatira* is the Roman Catholic Church of the Middle Ages, where love, faith, service, and perseverance were growing, but where falsehood was tolerated. Some people began to exalt the

(continued on page 50)

(continued from page 49)
Queen of Heaven (Mary) above the Son of God. Also, the Inquisition confiscated people's lands by charging them with heresy (compare Jezebel in 1 Kings 21:1-16).

5. *Sardis* is the Reformation Church, which emphasized names (denominations) and doctrines but was spiritually dead, despite its reputation for vitality.

6. *Philadelphia* is the missionary Church of the nineteenth and twentieth centuries.

7. *Laodicea* is the rich, complacent Church of the western world in the twentieth century.

1. Mounce, page 85.
2. Beasley-Murray, page 73.
3. F. F. Bruce, *Paul: Apostle of the Heart Set Free* (Grand Rapids, Michigan: William B. Eerdmans Publishing Company, 1977), page 291.
4. Charles Caldwell Ryrie, *Revelation* (Chicago: Moody Press, 1968), page 21.
5. Beasley-Murray, page 74.
6. Wilcock, page 45.
7. Beasley-Murray, page 80.
8. Mounce, page 91.
9. "The Martyrdom of Polycarp," *Early Christian Writings*, translated by Maxwell Staniforth (New York: Penguin Books, 1968), page 162.
10. Beasley-Murray, pages 82-83.
11. Beasley-Murray, page 84.
12. Mounce, page 96.
13. Ryrie, page 24.
14. Beasley-Murray, page 88.
15. Beasley-Murray, pages 89-90; Mounce, page 101.
16. Ryrie, page 26.
17. Mounce, pages 105-106.
18. Mounce, pages 108-109; Beasley-Murray, page 94.
19. Ryrie, page 27.
20. Beasley-Murray, page 99.
21. Ryrie, page 28.
22. *The NIV Study Bible*, page 1930.
23. Beasley-Murray, page 103.
24. Mounce, page 123.
25. Mounce, page 124.
26. Mounce, pages 125-126.
27. Beasley-Murray, page 105.
28. J. B. Smith, *A Revelation of Jesus Christ* (Scottsdale, Pennsylvania: Herald Press, 1961), page 61.

REVELATION 4:1-5:14

The Throne Room

Christians embroiled in persecution, temptation, and complacency need the kind of direct encouragement and rebuke Jesus gives in 2:1-3:22. Still, when you are up to your armpits in alligators, it's easy to forget that the heavenly perspective on the swamp is different from yours. In chapter 4, God begins to give us just such a heavenly view on earthly events. Whether these chapters describe events of the unspecified future or the eternal now, they are given to us to affect the way we deal with our circumstances today.

As you read 4:1-5:14, let God transport you to His throne room.

1. Chapters 4 and 5 are essentially an introduction to the action in chapters 6 through 20. Basically, what happens in 4:1-5:14?

   _____

   _____

   _____

   _____

   _____

   _____

   _____

For Thought and Discussion: Thrones, especially God's throne, are mentioned forty-five times in Revelation. Why do you think they appear so often? What do they have to do with the book's message?

For Thought and Discussion: a. What does the association between God and thunderstorms suggest to you about God?

b. Research the storm imagery in the Old Testament, beginning with Exodus 19:16-19.

Him who sits on the throne (4:1-11)

Jasper and carnelian (4:3). "Since God dwells in 'unapproachable light' and is one 'whom no one has seen or can see' (1 Timothy 6:16), he is described in terms of the reflected brilliance of precious stones."[1] Jasper varies in color, but it can be translucent like crystal (21:11). Carnelian (or sardius) is red.

A rainbow (4:3). In Genesis 9:12-17, God gives the rainbow as a sign of His faithfulness to His creation. One that fully encircles the throne (as opposed to the half-circle we see on earth) suggests utter faithfulness.

Twenty-four elders (4:4). Twenty-four divisions of priests and twenty-four of Levites led Israel's worship (1 Chronicles 24-25). The elders who lead worship in Heaven may be a special angelic order or twenty-four redeemed men who represent the whole of redeemed humanity before the throne. The number twenty-four is sometimes taken to be the sum of the twelve patriarchs (representing old Israel) and the twelve apostles (representing new Israel). *White* garments suggest holiness, and *crowns of gold* imply royalty.[2]

Lightning . . . thunder (4:5). In the Old Testament, God is revealed in a storm usually for judgment or salvation (1 Samuel 2:10, Job 37:13, Psalm 18:7-19). The appearance at Sinai (Exodus 19:7-25) sets the pattern for this awesome experience. In Revelation, each series of judgments concludes with lightning, thunder, and earthquake as God is about to be revealed in glory (Revelation 8:1-5, 11:19, 16:17-21). Here in chapter 4, it seems that "the power of holiness for wrath and redemption is inherent in the God of creation."[3]

Sea of glass (4:6). This probably represents God's holiness, which sets Him utterly apart even from those who dwell in Heaven.[4] It would also have the effect of reflecting the brilliant, gem-like light (4:3) around the Father and magnifying the awesome blaze.

Four living creatures (4:6). Among some two dozen interpretations are the following:

1. A Jewish tradition states that the eagle is the mightiest bird, the ox is the mightiest domesticated animal, the lion is the mightiest wild animal, the man is the mightiest of all, "and God has taken all these and secured them to His throne."[5] In this view, the four creatures "represent the entire animate creation."[6]

2. The creatures are "an exalted order of angelic beings who as the immediate guardians of the throne lead the heavenly hosts in adoration of God."[7]

Covered with eyes (4:6). This probably signifies unceasing vigilance.

Holy, holy, holy (4:8). In Hebrew, triple repetition was used for extreme emphasis.

Worship (4:10, 5:14). This Greek word originally meant to prostrate "oneself before deity to kiss his feet or the hem of his garment."[8] Thus, there is a double stress on falling down before the Lord in 4:10 and 5:14.

For Further Study: Compare the four creatures in Revelation to the angels in Isaiah 6:1-3 and Ezekiel 1:4-28.

For Thought and Discussion: What attitudes do you think are expressed by falling down before God? What is expressed by laying one's crown before Him?

Optional Application: Meditate this week on the vision of God in 4:1-11. Read and reread the chapter, letting it sink into you. Ponder how you should act towards such a God.

2. What impressions does 4:1-11 give you of God the Father? What can we learn about Him from this chapter?

_____

_____

_____

_____

_____

_____

3. a. From 4:1–5:14, what seems to be the number-one occupation in Heaven? (Consider especially 4:8-11, 5:8-14.)

_____

_____

For Thought and Discussion: What are your impressions of Heaven from 4:1-5:14?

b. Why is this important for us to know?

_____

_____

_____

_____

_____

4. For what reasons is the Father worthy of worship? Which of His deeds and attributes are praised in 4:8-11?

_____

_____

_____

_____

_____

The Lamb (5:1-14)

Scroll with writing on both sides (5:1). Papyrus (reed) scrolls were much more common for books than the modern form with pages. The fibers of papyrus ran horizontally on the front side of the scroll, which made writing easier than on the reverse side where the fibers ran vertically. Thus, the writing on both sides may mean that the scroll is filled to overflowing and sealed utterly to ensure its secrecy or inviolability until the proper time.

There were also other reasons for writing on both sides, such as with a contract deed. It was customary to write the terms of a contract on a sheet, fold it and seal it with seven seals to prevent tampering, and record the contents on the outside for reference.[9]

Lamb (5:6). Many Jewish apocalypses portray God's people as a flock out of which one arises to be the deliverer. He is called a lamb because he is

54

young. In these apocalypses, the victory of the conquering lamb has nothing to do with sacrifice or death. He conquers by strength. But God revealed to John the Baptist that the Messiah would be "the Lamb of God, who takes away the sin of the world" (John 1:29). This suggests the Jewish sacrificial system, especially the passover lamb (Exodus 12:1-14) or the lamb of Isaiah 53:7. The Lamb in Revelation reflects both of these images. John sees the Lamb *as if it had been slain*. The word means "having had his throat cut" in the manner of a sacrifice. However, He is *standing* as a victor.

Seven horns and seven eyes (5:6). In the Old Testament, the horn is a symbol for power, strength, or authority (Deuteronomy 33:17). Seven horns would symbolize full strength.[10] Seven eyes would represent full knowledge or wisdom—omniscience.[11]

Harp . . . incense (5:8). Normal features of Hebrew worship (Psalm 33:2, 141:2).

For Further Study: On Revelation 5:5, see Genesis 49:9 and Isaiah 11:1, both prophecies of the Messiah.

Optional Application: Meditate this week on what the Lamb has done for you. How should you respond? Thank Him for what He has done.

5. For what is the Lamb praised and worshiped (5:9-10,12-13)?

_____

_____

_____

_____

_____

6. How has He triumphed (5:5)? How has He purchased men for God with His blood (5:9)? (*Optional:* See John 19:16-37; Hebrews 9:11-14,22; 10:1-18; 1 John 2:1-2.)

_____

_____

_____

_____

7. How is this relevant to your life today?

_____

_____

_____

_____

_____

_____

8. Why do you think the Lamb's triumph makes Him worthy to open the seals on the scroll? (Consider what the scroll might be.)

_____

_____

_____

_____

_____

9. What can we learn about worship (its meaning, nature, reasons) from 4:1-5:14?

_____

_____

_____

_____

_____

_____

56

Your response

10. What one insight from 4:1–5:14 would you like to concentrate on for application this week?

_____

_____

_____

_____

_____

11. How have you already seen this truth at work in your life?

_____

_____

_____

_____

_____

12. In what new ways would you like it to affect you?

_____

_____

_____

_____

_____

13. What action can you take to cooperate with God in accomplishing this?

_____

_____

_____

_____

_____

14. List any questions you have about 4:1-5:14.

_____

_____

_____

_____

For the group

Warm-up. Discuss for a few minutes how each of you worships privately or in your church or fellowship. What does worship mean to you?

Read aloud. Ask someone to read these chapters with meaning. The songs, for example, should sound like praise.

Summarize. Question 1 is an opening summary question.

Questions. This lesson focuses on what God is like, what the Lamb has done, and worship. Question 8 is key for the whole book; you may find it less than obvious, but do take time to wrestle with it. It is what the Lamb has already accomplished that makes it possible for the rest of Revelation to take place. The future culmination of the Kingdom depends on the finished victory.

When the group understands this key truth and has examined what these chapters reveal about God, consider your own responses. Do you worship God with the same attitudes that you find in the elders and creatures (4:8,10; 5:14)? Have you ever been so overcome with God's majesty that you fell down and worshiped Him? If not physically, do you do this in your hearts? Discuss what worship means in light of 4:1-5:14.

Wrap-up.

Worship. These chapters are a fabulous springboard for worship. Praise God for the same attributes and deeds, and with the same attitudes, that you find in 4:1-5:14. Remember that the Greek for "worship" means to prostrate oneself before God's greatness.

The Millennium

Chapters 4 and 20 raise big debates among modern evangelicals. The controversies are over two concepts: *millennium* and *rapture*. We'll deal with the millennium here and the rapture on page 72.

The millennium is the thousand years described in 20:1-6. The name comes from Latin (*mille*="thousand" and *annus*="year"). There are three main views regarding the millennium:

1. *Premillennialism.* Christians experience both the Kingdom of God and tribulation today in a partial sense. However, at some point in the future the persecution and temptation will intensify into a Great Tribulation in which the beasts will arise, the two witnesses will testify, and the judgments of seals, trumpets, and bowls will occur. At the end of the Great Tribulation, Christ will return and defeat the enemy army at Armageddon. Then the faithful martyrs of the Tribulation (and/or the believers still alive, and/or all Christians) will be raised in the first resurrection. They will reign with Christ in "a literal, visible reign of peace and righteousness on the earth in space-time history."[12] That is the millennium. Afterward, the rest of the dead will be raised and judged. Finally, the old order will be replaced by a new heaven and earth, and the temporal Kingdom will be merged into the eternal Kingdom. This view is called *premillennial* because the Antichrist and the Tribulation come before (*pre-*) Christ's return and that occurs before the millennium. Premillennialists tend to take Revelation more literally, and its sequence more chronologically, than either postmillennialists or amillennialists. However, premillennialists cover a spectrum when interpreting the symbolism/plain meaning of particular verses and even whole chapters.

2. *Postmillennialism.* Our present experience of the Kingdom will grow and spread through evangelism and moral reform until eventually the whole world will be Christianized. Thus will come a long period of peace and prosperity, the millennium. Christ will return after (*post-*) the millennium and usher in the

(continued on page 60)

(continued from page 59)
resurrection, the last judgment, and the eternal Kingdom.

3. *Amillennialism.* A- means "not." That is, there will not be a special section of history called the millennium in the sense that pre- and postmillennialists believe. There are two slightly different approaches to amillennialism:

a. The events of 20:1-6 do not follow 19:11-21 (Christ's return) chronologically. They are a flashback. "The binding of Satan, the first resurrection, and the millennium are all metaphors for the present situation in this world, covering the period between the first and second comings of Christ. There is still to come the last revolt of evil, which is held to be the setting for such other predicted events as the great tribulation and the appearing of the man of lawlessness. It will be ended by Satan's overthrow and the judgment, which are described not only in 20:9-15 but also in 19:11-21."[13] The first resurrection is the believer's new birth, his rising to life after being dead in sin.

b. "The millennium describes the present reign of the souls of deceased believers with Christ in heaven. The present form of God's kingdom will be followed by Christ's return, the general resurrection, the final judgment and Christ's continuing reign over the perfect kingdom on the new earth in the eternal state."[14]

Confused? The commentaries listed on pages 163-164 may help you with the reasons behind each of these views.

1. *The NIV Study Bible*, page 1931.
2. Mounce, pages 135-136.
3. Beasley-Murray, page 115.
4. Beasley-Murray, page 116.
5. Beasley-Murray, page 117, quoting Rabbi Abahu, around 300 AD.
6. Beasley-Murray, page 117.
7. Mounce, page 138.
8. Mounce, page 139.
9. Beasley-Murray, pages 120-122.
10. *The NIV Study Bible*, page 1932; Beasley-Murray, page 124.
11. Beasley-Murray, page 124; Mounce, page 145.
12. *The NIV Study Bible*, page 1948.
13. Wilcock, page 179.
14. *The NIV Study Bible*, page 1948.

REVELATION 6:1-8:5

Seven Seals

Whatever the precise contents of the scroll—a contract, a will, God's plan for history—the important thing is that only the Lamb is worthy to open it and bring those contents into effect. His sacrificial death and resurrection have made Him worthy.

The inhabitants of Heaven are ecstatic that someone has been found who can open the scroll. The inhabitants of the earth are not so thrilled. Read (preferably aloud) what happens as the Lamb opens each of the seven seals in 6:1-8:5. Ask God to help you understand these visions.

Six seals (6:1-17)

1. What happens when the Lamb opens each of the first six seals?

1

2

For Further Study:
To keep track of where you are in Revelation, it is a good idea to look back at your outline on pages 15-16 frequently. You can change the outline as you go along, if you like.

3

_____

4

_____

5

_____

6

_____

White horse . . . rider (6:2). The imagery of the four horsemen in 6:2-8 comes from Zechariah 1:8-17, 6:1-8. In the Old Testament, horses were rarely used for peaceful purposes; they suggested war to the Jewish mind.

The rider on the white horse has been thought to be Christ because of 19:11, but the descriptions are not very similar (even the words for "crown" are different). Other suggestions are the triumph of evangelism in the world, the Antichrist, and the spirit of conquest and militarism. (See the commentaries for reasons.)

Followers of the preterist view (see pages 31-32) think the first five seals represent events of Roman times: invasion by the Parthians (who customarily used bows); warfare by Rome's

62

armies; the famine of 62 AD; the pestilence that followed Rome's wars; the persecution of Nero.[1]

Robert Mounce notes that the events of the seals happen in preparation for the opening of the scroll. This, he says, means that the seal-judgments represent what has been happening since John's time in preparation for the very last things, which begin with the trumpets (8:2).[2]

Other scholars observe parallels between the seals and the "beginning of birthpangs" (Matthew 24:8) Jesus foretold. These may be the characteristic events of the Church age or an intensification of them before the Great Tribulation.

Strict futurists, including dispensationalists, hold that the seals are as much in the future as the trumpets and bowls.

For Thought and Discussion: Do you think the four horsemen represent judgments God has been sending throughout the last days? Do you think they refer specifically to the last few years before Jesus' return? Explain your reasoning.

2. From the descriptions in 6:2-8, what do you think each of the four horsemen represents?

white _____

_____

red _____

_____

black _____

_____

pale _____

_____

3. What do the judgments wrought by the four horsemen have in common?

_____

_____

_____

_____

_____

Optional Application: Could you say that your life thus far has been a sacrificial offering to God? Think about and meditate on Romans 12:1 and 2 Timothy 4:6, looking for ways to live like those poured out on the altar of God.

4. Jesus gave His own discourse on the end times in Matthew 24:4-51 (paralleled in Mark 13:1-37 and Luke 21:5-31). What does Jesus say about wars and famines in Matthew 24:4-8?

_____

_____

_____

_____

_____

Under the altar (6:9). The place where the blood of sacrifices was poured out (Exodus 29:12). Of course, Christ's blood was the sufficient sacrifice (Revelation 5:9), but even Paul describes his ministry as a self-offering to God (Philippians 3:7-8, 2 Timothy 4:6). The altar is also a place of honor, in the very presence of God.

5. The fifth seal is an interlude rather than a judgment (6:9-11). What is the answer to the martyrs' question in 6:10?

_____

_____

_____

_____

6. Revelation 6:10-11 was an important insight into heavenly reality for John's first-century readers enduring persecution. Why is this an important insight for you and other modern Christians?

_____

_____

_____

_____

For Further Study:
How does Revelation
6:12-17 fulfill Isaiah
2:6-22?

Earthquake . . . sun . . . moon (6:12). In Jesus'
discourse on the last days, these events seem to
immediately precede the Second Coming (Matthew 24:29-31, Mark 13:24-27, Luke 21:25-28).
Some futurists conclude that this is the end
before the Second Coming, and that the
trumpets and bowls look at the same period of
time from different vantage points. Such people
point out that it would be hard for 6:12-14 to
both literally and chronologically precede 8:12.[3]

Those who think the seals will precede the
trumpets chronologically say the earthquake,
blackening of the sun, reddening of the moon,
and receding of the sky will be temporary. The
falling of the stars is a meteor shower.[4] Jesus'
discourse in Matthew 24 describes only the
period of the seals, then skips to the Second
Coming.

Many Old Testament prophets predict the
earthquake, darkness, etc., as signs of the day of
the Lord (Isaiah 2:10-22, 34:4; Ezekiel 32:7-8;
Joel 2:10,30-31; etc.). These events are also
common to most apocalypses. For these reasons,
some interpreters argue that the predictions
should be taken more symbolically than literally,
while others think they are simply well attested.

7. How will people—mighty and lowly—react to
the sixth seal's judgment (6:15-17)?

_____

_____

_____

_____

8. How is this a warning or an encouragement to
you?

_____

_____

_____

_____

For Further Study:
Do some research to decide for yourself who you think the 144,000 and the great multitude are.

The 144,000 and the great multitude (7:1-17)

Before we find out what happens when the seventh seal is opened, John's vision is interrupted. The sixth seal brought such a cataclysm that we might wonder what happens to believers. Two visions in chapter 7 give us glimpses.

9. What happens in . . .

7:1-8? _____

_____

_____

_____

7:9-17? _____

_____

_____

_____

Seal (7:3). "Ancient documents were folded and tied, and a lump of clay was pressed over the knot. The sender would then stamp the hardening clay with his signet ring or roll it with a cylinder seal, which authenticated and protected the contents. The sealing in chapter 7 results in the name of the Lord being stamped on the forehead of his followers (see 9:4; 14:1; compare 22:4). Its primary purpose is to protect the people of God in the coming judgments. For the background, see Ezekiel 9:4, where the mark was the Hebrew letter *Taw*, made like an X or a +."[5]

144,000 (7:4). "Some find here a reference to members of actual Jewish tribes, the faithful Jewish remnant of the 'great tribulation'" (7:14).[6] Those who hold this view generally think Gentile believers will be taken to Heaven ("raptured"—see page 72) before the tribulation starts, so the only believers on earth are newly-

66

converted thousands of Jews. These alone
require sealing because they alone are left to
face the onslaught.

"Others take the passage as symbolic of all
the faithful believers who live during the period
of tribulation."[7] Interpreters who do not think
all Gentile believers will be raptured before the
tribulation generally say God will surely seal all
the believers left on earth. On this reading,
144,000 is not a literal statistic but a symbol:
12 x 12 x 10 x 10 x 10 (see pages 104-106).

Idealists and amillennialists (the two are
often the same) think the 144,000 are all Christians in all generations, who have been sealed
by the Holy Spirit (Ephesians 1:13-14) to protect them from ultimate destruction.

Great multitude (7:9). Those who think Gentile
believers will be raptured before the tribulation
see these as Gentiles and Jews converted during
the tribulation (7:14) by the witness of the
sealed Jews of 7:1-8.

Those who think Gentile believers will not
be raptured beforehand (including some premillennialists and all post- and amillennialists)
equate the great multitude with the 144,000:
Christians who remain faithful through the
tribulation and "come out" (7:14) at death or
the Second Coming.

Palm branches (7:9). The Jews carried these in festival celebrations as symbols of joy and victory.[8]

10. Why is it important for us to know that . . .

God's servants will be sealed before God afflicts
the land and the sea with the final judgments
(7:3)?

_____

_____

_____

_____

_____

67

For Thought and Discussion: Why do you think the opening of the last seal is interrupted by the two visions of chapter 7? What purpose do they serve at this point in the story?

the robes of the great multitude will be made white in the blood of the Lamb as they come through and out of the tribulation (7:14)?

_____

_____

_____

_____

the multitude will serve God day and night in His temple (7:15)?

_____

_____

_____

_____

11. What personal relevance and encouragement do you find in 7:16-17?

_____

_____

_____

_____

_____

The seventh seal (8:1-5)

12. What happens when the Lamb opens the seventh seal (8:1-5)?

_____

_____

_____

_____

Silence (8:1). This has been called a silence of "expectancy" and "foreboding."[9] It may also be a stillness while God hears the **the prayers of all the saints** (8:3).[10]

Incense (8:3). In 5:8, the incense *is* (represents) the prayers of the saints. This is a possible rendering of the Greek in 8:3.[11] Alternatively, the incense may symbolize the sweet smell of sacrifice (the work of Christ) that accompanies the prayers and makes them acceptable.[12] Incense was burned in a **censer**, a firepan that held burning charcoal.

For Thought and Discussion: A hush suddenly falls (8:1) after the thundering judgment and praise of chapters 6 and 7. How would you feel in John's place, seeing this?

13. When the seventh seal is opened, there is first silence, then prayer. How do you interpret the heavenly response to the saints' prayers (8:5)?

_____

_____

_____

_____

14. What can we learn about the following from 6:1-8:5?

the Father _____

_____

_____

_____

_____

Christ _____

_____

_____

_____

_____

the Kingdom of God _____

_____

_____

_____

_____

suffering and endurance _____

_____

_____

_____

Your response

15. What one insight from 6:1–8:5 would you like to take to heart this week?

_____

_____

_____

_____

16. How would you like this truth to affect your life?

_____

_____

_____

_____

17. What action can you take to allow this to happen, by God's grace?

_____

_____

_____

_____

18. List any questions you have about 6:1-8:5.

_____

_____

_____

_____

For the group

Warm-up. Ask group members to share briefly how 4:1-5:14 has affected their worship or another aspect of their relationships with God. Has anyone seen any other effects on his or her life?

Read aloud and summarize.

Questions. Interpreting the visions of 6:1-8:5 for yourselves is not easy. The differences among scholars should be sufficient warning of this. Try to avoid arguments, but encourage group members to state their views clearly and support them sensibly. In an effort to be brief, the notes in this and later lessons may seem confusing or insufficient. If so, ask some group members to consult one or more commentaries and report to the group on their findings.

Emphasize application. Despite differences among interpretations, commentators agree remarkably as to how we should respond to these visions. Whether or not we are the 144,000 or the great multitude, these visions have implications for our actions and attitudes. Likewise, even if 6:1-17 describes the distant future, it still has relevance to the present. You don't have to be an idealist to find present applications of Revelation.

Wrap-up.

Worship. Praise God for His responses to the cries and prayers of the saints, "How long, Sovereign Lord, holy and true, until you judge the inhabitants of the earth and avenge our blood?" (6:10). Praise Him that the seals will be opened and judgment will come. Thank Him for the sealing of His servants and for the joy of those who come out of the Great Tribulation.

The Rapture

This is the event in which believers on earth "will be caught up together with them [members of the Church who have died] in the clouds to meet the Lord in the air" (1 Thessalonians 4:17). Nearly all evangelicals believe that a literal rapture will occur before Christ's Second Coming. However, they disagree about how long before.

Pre-tribulation premillennialists believe Christians will be raptured just before the beginning of the Great Tribulation. Their departure will cause many nonChristians (including 144,000 Jews) to put faith in Christ and become the martyrs of the tribulation.

Mid-tribulation premillennialists believe Christians will be raptured in the middle of the seven-year tribulation.

Post-tribulation premillennialists think Christians will be raptured at the end of the tribulation, just as Christ is returning to begin His thousand-year reign on earth.

Amillennialists believe Christians will be raptured just as Christ is returning to inaugurate His reign in the new heavens and new earth.

Many pre-tribulation premillenialists are called *dispensationalists* because they believe God deals with believers differently in different dispensations. For instance, He dealt with Israel (believers after Abraham and before Christ) one way. He deals with the Church (believers alive between Christ's resurrection and the rapture) another way. He will have another dispensation for believers during the Great Tribulation.

1. Beasley-Murray, page 132, note 1. Beasley-Murray gives his reasons for rejecting this view.
2. Mounce, page 151.
3. Beasley-Murray, pages 137-138.
4. Ryrie, pages 47-48.
5. *The NIV Study Bible*, page 1934.
6. *The NIV Study Bible*, page 1934.
7. *The NIV Study Bible*, page 1934.
8. Mounce, page 171; Beasley-Murray, page 146.
9. Ryrie, page 55.
10. Beasley-Murray, pages 149-150.
11. *The NIV Study Bible*, page 1935.
12. Ryrie, page 56; Beasley-Murray, pages 150-151.

REVELATION 8:6-9:21

Six Trumpets

When the seventh seal was opened, the scroll was ready to be unrolled, read, and put into effect. At that moment, Heaven fell silent. Seven angels were given trumpets. The prayers of the saints went up before God, and in response, fire was cast upon the earth. The thunder of judgment rumbled. With that warning, the trumpets are blown.

Read 8:6-9:21 carefully and prayerfully, observing what happens when each trumpet sounds.

Trumpets (8:6). Trumpets that herald the end of the age are a tradition "with roots deep in the history of Israel." Trumpets were used to warn the people of an emergency and to summon them to battle, so it was natural for the prophets to use them as a symbol to warn the people of approaching judgment (Ezekiel 33:1-6, Joel 2:1). Trumpets were also used to herald gladness, festivals, the new year, and the season of repentance leading up to the Day of Atonement (Leviticus 23:24, Numbers 10:10). So Joel 2:12-17 uses the trumpet as a call to an assembly of repentance to turn judgment into mercy. Finally, the trumpet on the last day heralds the deliverance of God's people (Zechariah 9:14) and therefore the resurrection (Matthew 24:31, 1 Corinthians 15:52, 1 Thessalonians 4:16). "Judgment, repentance, deliverance, salvation, new age heralded by the trumpet sound call to mind the use of the trumpet in ancient Israel to proclaim the accession of a king to the throne" (1 Kings 1:39; Psalm 47:5, 98:6). Just as trumpets preceded God's self-revelation at Sinai (Exodus 19:11-13), so the Jews expected His appearance at the end of the age to be heralded with trumpets.

All this and more may be behind God's choice of trumpets to launch this series of judgments on the earth's inhabitants.[1]

1. Briefly describe what happens in each stage of 8:6-9:19.

8:6-7 _____

_____

_____

_____

8:8-9 _____

_____

_____

_____

8:10-11 _____

_____

_____

_____

8:12 _____

_____

_____

_____

8:13 _____

_____

_____

9:1-12 _____

_____

_____

_____

_____

9:13-19 _____

_____

_____

_____

For Further Study:
God sent plagues on Egypt to deliver His people from slavery, reveal His power, judge the Egyptians for idolatry, and prove that the gods of Egypt were false. Compare the plagues in Exodus 7:14-11:10 to the judgments of trumpets and bowls in Revelation. What echoes of Exodus do you observe in Revelation? What do you think God is saying by planning these echoes?

Wormwood (8:11). "A plant with a strong, bitter taste. . . . It is used here as a metaphor for calamity and sorrow. . . . It is not poisonous, but its bitterness suggests death."[2]

Star that had fallen (9:1). The star in 8:10 is apparently "part of a cosmic disturbance," but "here the star is a divine agent, probably an angel."[3] He is an evil angel, **the angel of the Abyss** (9:11) whose name in both Hebrew and Greek is Destroyer. Some people say he is Satan (see Isaiah 14:12-13, Luke 10:18).

The Abyss (9:1-2,11). This is the deep, the bottomless pit, which the ancients thought of as the abode of demons.

2. The first four seals were limited judgment: oil and wine were spared from the famine (6:6); only a fourth of humanity died (6:8). How do the first four trumpets compare (8:7-12)?

_____

_____

_____

_____

75

For Thought and Discussion: In your judgment, is it right for Christians to pray that God will judge the wicked? Why or why not? If so, with what attitude should we do this?

3. Compare what the martyrs said about the inhabitants of the earth after the fifth seal was opened (6:10) to what the eagle says about the inhabitants before the fifth trumpet (8:13). What do you observe?

_____

_____

_____

_____

_____

4. Along the same lines, consider how God responds to the prayers of the saints (8:3-5). What have the saints apparently prayed?

_____

_____

_____

_____

_____

5. a. How do the inhabitants of the earth respond to the horrible but still limited plagues of the first six trumpets (9:20-21)?

_____

_____

_____

_____

   b. What does this tell you about human character?

_____

_____

_____

_____

c. Have you seen this attitude today? If so, explain.

_____

_____

_____

_____

For Further Study: In many of His judgments, God afflicts nature in order to warn and punish humans. Why do you think He does this? See Genesis 2-3 and Deuteronomy 28.

6. Only a third of the earth, the trees, the sea creatures, the drinking water, the sun, etc., are affected by the first four trumpets. The locusts are allowed to torture but not to kill (9:5). The four angels are permitted to kill only a third of mankind (9:15). Why do you think God sends such horrifying plagues, yet limits them? (Consider 9:20-21.)

For Thought and Discussion: What do you think the locusts of 9:1-12 are? Literal locusts? Demons? Symbolic of the torments of life that make unbelievers want to die? Explain your reasoning.

_____

_____

_____

_____

7. Do you think God is cruel to send such awful afflictions on the inhabitants of the earth? Why or why not?

_____

_____

_____

_____

8. What difference does it make to you that the locusts are freed with God's permission (9:1) and that God chooses what they are and aren't allowed to do (9:3-5)?

_____

_____

_____

_____

_____

9. How are the visions of the first six trumpets
   relevant to us in our time? What lessons do they
   have for us (about God, the Kingdom, suffering,
   patient endurance, ultimate reality)?

_____

_____

_____

_____

_____

Your response

10. How would you like what you have seen in
    8:6-9:21 to affect your life?

_____

_____

_____

_____

11. Are there any steps you can take to help bring
    this about? If so, describe them.

_____

_____

_____

_____

12. List any questions you have about 8:6-9:21.

_____

_____

_____

_____

For the group

Warm-up. Ask, "What does the sound of a trumpet call suggest to you? What feelings and expectations does it give you?"

Read aloud and summarize.

Questions. We have deliberately given little space to figuring out what the blazing mountain or the locust-creatures "really are." Our reasons are: 1) There is such widespread disagreement that arguments are likely; 2) if the events are future and cataclysmic, we shouldn't expect to understand them ahead of time. Feel free to discuss whether you think the trumpet judgments symbolize present or future realities, and what each means. But don't spend so much time on this that you lose track of the main points: Why is God doing this? What do these actions reveal about Him? How should they affect our choices and actions in the present? Most of the questions in this lesson hinge on these.

Summarize and wrap-up.

Worship. Praise God for being in control even when Satan is loosed to do his worst. Praise Him for having reasons for and limits on even the ultimate judgments that ravage the earth. Thank Him for protecting His servants from the most horrible afflictions (9:4) and for limiting the plagues so that all mankind has the chance to repent. Thank Him for hearing and answering the prayers of the saints for justice. Ask Him to motivate you to act on the warning and promise of the trumpets.

1. Beasley-Murray, pages 152-155. Wilcock, pages 85-100, presents an idealist's view of the trumpets that we have not tried to give in notes. He sees the trumpets as representing judgments that God is even now meting out to those who refuse to repent.
2. *The NIV Study Bible*, page 1935.
3. *The NIV Study Bible*, page 1936.

REVELATION 10:1-11:19

The Seventh Trumpet

You might have thought people would repent of their rebellious wickedness after the first six trumpets, but their twisted hearts only found in the warnings more reasons for hatred. The plagues have mounted to awful heights; mankind is unchastened; we are poised for the final blast.

But as we paused after the sixth seal to learn what was happening to the Church in the midst of it all, so we pause after the sixth trumpet to hear God's Word about His prophets and witnesses. Read 10:1-11:19 carefully, asking God to unfold to you the significance of these visions.

The angel and the scroll (10:1-11)

In Daniel 10:4-12:13, a mighty angel appears to Daniel with a "face like lightning, his eyes like flaming torches, his arms and legs like the gleam of burnished bronze, and his voice like the sound of a multitude" (10:6). He predicts to Daniel what history holds for the next several centuries (11:1-35), then shifts to foretell the end of the age (11:36-12:4). After this prophecy, Daniel sees two other angels, one of whom asks, "How long will it be before these astonishing things are fulfilled?" (12:6). The first angel raises his hands toward Heaven and swears "by him who lives forever and ever, saying, 'It will be for a time, times, and half a time. When the power of the holy people has finally broken, then all these things will be completed'" (12:7).

81

Mystery of God (Revelation 10:7). Recall that in biblical terms, a "mystery" is a plan that God has kept secret but has now revealed. In this verse, the mystery "is that God has won the victory over the forces of evil and will reign forever and ever" (11:15).[1] The mystery is "the completion of God's purpose in creation."[2]

1. How is the vision of Revelation 10:1-7 like that of Daniel 10:4–12:13 described above?

_____

_____

_____

_____

2. In Daniel 12:5-7, one angel asks, "How long?" In Revelation 6:9-11, the martyrs ask, "How long?" How is the angel's oath in 10:6-7 different from the oath in Daniel 12:7 and the answer in Revelation 6:11?

Daniel 12:5-7, Revelation 6:9-11	Revelation 10:6-7

3. In light of Daniel 12:6-7 and Revelation 6:9-11, why do you think there is now no more delay before God's purpose is accomplished?

_____

_____

_____

4. Why is the oath of Revelation 10:6-7 important for us to know about?

_____

_____

_____

_____

For Thought and Discussion: Why is it significant that God sent His angel to swear by Him, the eternal Creator of everything, that there would be no more delay? (See Hebrews 6:16-20.)

For Thought and Discussion: Have God's words ever tasted sweet in your mouth but upset your stomach when you digested them? Why does this happen?

Announced (10:7). The Greek word *euengelisen* is related to *euangelion*, the good news or gospel. God "gospeled" His secret purpose ahead of time to the prophets. (Compare Amos 3:7.)

Little scroll (10:2,9). Not the scroll of chapter 5, but one containing some or all of the prophecies John will have to digest and proclaim.

5. What do you think is symbolized by John's eating the scroll of God's words and finding it sweet in his mouth and sour in his stomach (10:9-11)?

_____

_____

_____

6. What lesson or message for us does 10:9-11 offer?

_____

_____

_____

_____

Two witnesses (11:1-14)

Your interpretation of chapter 11 depends a great deal on how you understand the book's language. One approach takes the material in its plainest, most literal way possible: the Jewish Temple will be rebuilt in or just before the tribulation; the ancient sacrifices will be renewed on the altar; the two witnesses are two individuals. Another view takes the chapters symbolically: "the temple is the church, the two witnesses are that part of the church which must suffer martyrdom, and the great city represents civilization utterly alien to the will of God."[3]

Among conservative evangelicals, the debate is not about whether or not the Scripture is true. Those who prefer the literal or "plain" meaning think we should interpret Revelation in much the same way that we interpret a narrative like Acts. They point out that biblical people generally interpret prophecies literally. (For example, in Daniel 9:2, Daniel takes literally the seventy years Jeremiah prophesied in Jeremiah 25:11-12, 29:10.) Those who take Revelation symbolically say that because it is written as an apocalypse, we should interpret it according to the rules of apocalyptic. We will leave this decision to you. The questions that follow emphasize what you can learn from John's vision regardless of exactly how you think it will be fulfilled.

Reed (11:1). In the Old Testament, Jerusalem and the Temple are measured with a view to either destruction or restoration (Isaiah 34:11; Ezekiel 40:1-42:20; Zechariah 1:16, 2:1-5).

Temple (11:1). The Greek word *naos* refers to the Holy of Holies, the innermost sanctuary where God dwelt in the Temple that existed during John's lifetime (it was destroyed in 70 AD). It may also include the courts to which Israelites, God's people, were admitted. Outside those courts was the court of the Gentiles.

42 months (11:2). Three and a half years. Daniel 9:24-27 prophesied that the remainder of history would be divided into seventy "weeks" of years. Sixty-nine of those years would elapse between

84

the decree to rebuild Jerusalem (445 BC?; Nehemiah 2:1) and the coming of the Messiah as King (30 BC?).[4] Then the Messiah would be "cut off" (Daniel 9:26). Some scholars conclude that the seventieth week is the time of Jesus' earthly ministry and immediately thereafter, others take it as the Church Age, others as the whole span of history, and others as the last literal seven years of history (see commentaries on Daniel).

The seventieth week is divided into two equal parts of three and a half years each (Daniel 9:27). This is called "a time, times, and half a time" in Daniel 7:25, 12:7; and Revelation 12:14. It is called 1,260 days in Revelation 11:3 and 12:6. Some interpreters understand the three and a half years the way it is used in apocalyptic, as "a conventional symbol for a limited period of unrestrained wickedness."[5] Others understand it as a literal three and a half years of the "Great Tribulation." Others take it as representing the Church Age, all of history since Christ "put an end to sacrifice and offering" (Daniel 9:27).

This is all highly technical and much debated. What you should glean from it is that the forty-two months/three and a half years/1,260 days of Revelation each correspond to half of the seventieth week of Daniel.[6] It is agreed by all interpreters that the three and a half years is either half or all of the period of tribulation.

---

7. What do you think the measuring of the Temple but not the court of the Gentiles represents (11:1-2)?

_____

_____

_____

8. Why is it important for us to know that the Temple is measured before the city is given over to be trampled (11:1-2)? What do you think is the relevance for us?

_____

_____

_____

Sackcloth (11:3). "A coarse, dark cloth woven from the hair of goats or camels. It was worn as a sign of mourning and penitence (Joel 1:13; Jonah 3:5-6; Matthew 11:21)."[7]

Olive trees (11:4). In Zechariah 4:1-14, the two olive trees or olive branches are two anointed leaders who supply oil (the Holy Spirit) to the lampstand (probably the nation of Israel). The leaders are probably the king and the high priest who foreshadow the Priest-King, the Messiah (Zechariah 6:13).[8] In Revelation, the two olive trees (bearers of the Spirit) are *the two lampstands*. Since in Revelation 1:20 lampstands equal churches, the *two witnesses* (11:3) are either the church, part of the church (the martyrs), or two individuals who as leaders fulfill the church's mission to be Christ's witnesses (Mark 13:10).

Jewish law required two witnesses to confirm the guilt of a criminal (Deuteronomy 19:15). These two in Revelation have the power of Elijah to devour their enemies with fire and cause drought (Revelation 11:5-6, 1 Kings 17:1, 2 Kings 1:10-12). They have the power of Moses to turn water into blood and cause other plagues (Exodus 7:17-21). Like Moses and Elijah, they are prophets (Revelation 11:3); they declare God's word of judgment and urge repentance to the corrupt world.

Beast (11:7). This is the first mention of this figure, who is the chief enemy of God in the last days (13:1-18, 17:7-11).

Lie in the street (11:8). In the Near East, a decent burial was usually considered so important that it was provided even for enemies. To deny burial was the worst possible insult and outrage.

Great city (11:8). It is called **Sodom** because that city symbolized immorality (Genesis 19:4-11) and **Egypt** because that nation represented slavery and oppression. The **Lord was crucified** in Jerusalem, but some people think this could equally be Rome because Roman power was the immediate cause of Jesus' execution. In 17:1-18:24 the great city is described as Babylon. All of these names may be figurative, comparing the world opposed to God to the worst cities of history. Alternatively, one or more of the city names may be literal. There is disagreement as to whether or not "the great city" in 11:8, 16:19, and 17:18 refers to the same city.

For Thought and Discussion: a. What does 11:1-14 tell us about God?

b. What does it tell us about the world?

For Thought and Discussion: To what extent is every Christian's responsibility and protection like those of the two witnesses? (See Luke 12:8-12, 21:12-19.)

9. Recall how people responded to the first six trumpet-plagues (9:20-21). How does three and a half years of testimony from the two witnesses affect these people (11:3-12)?

_____

_____

_____

_____

10. What encouragement for Christians even now does the story of the two witnesses offer?

_____

_____

_____

_____

_____

Gave glory to the God of heaven (11:13). As in Joshua 7:19 and Jeremiah 13:16, this may mean that many survivors glorify God by repenting of their sin. Alternatively, it may mean that the survivors realize in terror that the Christ whom they have reviled, not the Antichrist whom they have worshiped, is the true Lord of the universe (compare 6:15-17, 13:4).

87

For Thought and Discussion: Decide for yourself in which of the two ways you think mankind will "give glory to the God of heaven" when the two witnesses are resurrected and the earthquake destroys a tenth of the city. What does this reaction to miracle and disaster tell you about human nature?

For Thought and Discussion: Earlier, God was called Him "who is, and who was, and who is to come" (1:4,8; 4:8). Why do you suppose "who is to come" is dropped in 11:17?

The seventh trumpet (11:15-17)

11. We might have expected the seventh trumpet to usher in the third woe (8:13; 9:1,12-13; 11:14). Instead, we get a heavenly chorus of joy. What do you think this signifies? Why is Heaven singing when we still have six chapters before John describes the return of Christ?

_____

_____

_____

_____

12. Reflect on what the hosts of Heaven sing. How is it relevant to you that . . .

"The kingdom of the world has become the kingdom of our Lord and of his Christ, and he will reign for ever and ever" (11:15)?

_____

_____

_____

_____

"The time has come for judging the dead . . . and for destroying those who destroy the earth" (11:18)?

_____

_____

_____

"The time has come . . . for rewarding your servants the prophets and your saints and those who reverence your name, both small and great" (11:18)?

_____

_____

_____

Your response

13. What one insight from 10:1-11:18 would you like to take to heart this week?

_____

_____

_____

14. How would you like it to affect your life in deeper ways?

_____

_____

_____

15. What action can you take along these lines?

_____

_____

_____

_____

16. List any questions you have about 10:1-11:18.

_____

_____

_____

For Thought and Discussion: How can the heavenly host speak of "our Lord and of his Christ" as "he" (11:15)? Does "he" refer to the Father, Christ, or both?

Optional Application: Thank and worship God for the truths declared in 11:18. How should these truths affect your priorities and actions?

For the group

Warm-up. Ask, "Do you ever wish the Lord would hurry up and fulfill His promises to bring justice to the earth? Do you ever pray, 'Come, Lord Jesus' with a sense of urgency or impatience? Or, are you content to have things go on as they are?" Be prepared for a wide variety of responses to this question. Encourage group members to say how they really feel, not how they think they should. You might even ask, "How do you think we *should* feel?"

Read aloud and summarize.

Questions. Let everyone state how he or she views 11:1-14. (Is this about the present or the future? Are the witnesses individuals or the Church?) However, don't let a debate take over your discussion. Instead, what exhortation or encouragement to action and attitude can you derive from 10:1-11:18? How should each of you live in light of these visions?

If group members have questions like, "What did the seven thunders of 10:3-4 say?" consult commentaries. There are innumerable good questions that this study does not attempt to address. Likewise, members might want to research various views on the measuring of the Temple, the identities of the two witnesses, the great city, or the seventh trumpet and report back to the group. Be careful not to let your study deteriorate into an intellectual exercize.

Summarize and wrap-up.

Worship. John's visions can prompt worship. Use songs that express the joy of the seventh trumpet. Praise God for the oath that when the time is ripe (now?) there will be no more delay in the accomplishing of the mystery of the gospel. Praise Him for sending prophets to digest and proclaim His words, even at the cost of their lives. Thank Him that though the wicked kill His witnesses, He will raise them to glory. Praise Him that even before all is accomplished, the heavenly chorus can declare His victory and reign. Praise Him that the time for judging the dead and rewarding the saints will come.

1. *The NIV Study Bible*, page 1937.
2. Beasley-Murray, page 174.
3. Mounce, page 218.
4. These dates use the lunar calendar of the Jews. There is an alternate calculation using the solar calendar. The issue is highly technical; see commentaries on Daniel.
5. *The NIV Study Bible*, page 1938.
6. Some people think 11:2-3 refers to the first half of the final seven years, while 12:6,14 (and all of chapter 13) refers to the second half. That is, the two witnesses testify for 1,260 days, then Satan falls, then the woman of chapter 12 is driven into the wilderness, then Satan makes war on her offspring by sending the beasts of chapter 13 for another 1,260 days. Others think all of this happens during the same period of time. See the commentaries for details of this whole debate.
7. *The NIV Study Bible*, page 1938.
8. *The NIV Study Bible*, pages 1410-1411.

REVELATION 12:1-13:18

A Woman, a Dragon, and Two Beasts

When a door was opened in Heaven, John saw the throne room with thunder rumbling and lightning flashing from the throne (4:1-5). When the Lamb opened the seventh seal, Heaven fell silent, the saints' prayers were offered, and fire was cast on the earth with more thunder and lightning (8:1-5). When the seventh trumpet was blown, not silence but a chorus of celebration erupted in Heaven, and God's temple—His throne room—was once again opened with crashes and flashes of the divine storm (11:19).

With the final trumpet, we might have expected the third and most devastating woe, the return of Christ, and the consummation of the Kingdom. Instead, chapters 12 through 14 give us a series of visions about the conflict between the Church and the powers of evil—war in Heaven and war on earth. The whole reason why the seven churches are suffering, why John is on Patmos, why the witnesses must be martyred in the last days is explained in these chapters. Likewise, these visions explain why the seals and trumpets, as well as the bowls yet to come, are necessary.

Read 12:1-13:18 carefully. Ask God to enable you to understand the cosmic struggle between holy and evil, and "the suffering and kingdom and patient endurance that are ours in Christ Jesus" (1:9).

1. Briefly describe what John sees in each of the following passages:

12:1-6 _____

_____

_____

_____

_____

12:7-12 _____

_____

_____

_____

_____

12:13-13:1 _____

_____

_____

_____

_____

13:2-10 _____

_____

_____

_____

13:11-18 _____

_____

_____

_____

_____

_____

The woman, the dragon, and the male child (12:1-6)

Sign (12:1,3; 15:1). "An extraordinary spectacle or event that points beyond itself" (compare Luke 21:11,25; Acts 2:19).[1]

A woman (12:1). The faithful nation of Israel, who gave birth to the Messiah, the *male child* of 12:5. Her other *offspring* (12:17) are the Christian (Jewish and Gentile) believers, for after Jesus' resurrection faithful Israel becomes the Church.[2] Zion as the mother of God's people is a familiar image in the Bible (Isaiah 66:7-11, Galatians 4:26).

Red dragon (12:3). Many nations of John's day had stories about dragons. The dragon came to symbolize evil; in Jewish writings it is the archenemy of God. Verse 9 identifies this dragon. His *seven heads and ten horns* (12:3) suggest the perfection of (wicked) wisdom and power. His *seven crowns* "are not wreaths of victory but 'crowns of arrogated authority.'"[3]

The woman fled (12:6). The woman's protection in the *desert* is further elaborated in 12:13-17. In Old Testament terms, the desert often represents not a wasteland, "but a place of spiritual refuge" (1 Kings 17:2-6, Hosea 2:14).[4] As Israel fled into the desert to escape slavery in Egypt, and Mary and Joseph fled there to escape Herod's attempt to kill Jesus (Matthew 2:13-18), and the Christians of Jerusalem (including John) fled there to escape the city's destruction in 70 AD, so the Church flees there from Satan's onslaught during the three and a half years.

---

2. In your own words, explain what you think is the meaning of John's vision in 12:1-6.

_____

_____

_____

_____

_____

_____

War in Heaven (12:7-12)

The vision of the earthly struggle between the woman and the dragon is interrupted by a glimpse of the parallel heavenly war.

Michael (12:7). The only angel explicitly called an archangel in the Bible (Daniel 10:13,21; 12:1; Jude 9). In Daniel 12:1, he is the prince who will protect Israel in the final conflict. He, not Christ, is the heavenly counterpart of Satan: Michael is the archangel over God's angels, and Satan is the archangel over his evil angels (Matthew 25:41). Both Michael and Satan rank below the Son of God. Thus, it is fitting that Michael leads the heavenly battle against Satan after Christ has won the decisive victory through His death and resurrection (Revelation 12:5,11).

   Although Satan was a morally "fallen" angel before the earth's creation, he has still had access to God's throne room to accuse men and women (Job 1:6-12, 2:1-6). In the heavenly war made possible by the victory on the Cross, Satan is **hurled to the earth** (Revelation 12:9)— barred from making accusations in Heaven. Some interpreters think this defeat occurred at the time of Christ's death and resurrection, and that now Satan has lost his power to accuse us (12:10-12) but can still persecute us (12:12,17). Others think the defeat will occur at the beginning or in the midst of the final Great Tribulation, and that Satan is presently still able to accuse us before God.

Devil, or Satan (12:9). _Devil_ is Greek for "slanderer." _Satan_ is Hebrew for "adversary." Both names imply **accuser** (12:10)—a legal adversary who slanderously accuses someone in court.

3. What can we learn about Satan (his character, activities, and destiny) from 12:7-12?

_____

_____

_____

_____

_____

_____

4. a. Who are "they" in 12:11 who have overcome the accuser? (Consider 12:10-11.)

_____

_____

b. How have they overcome Satan? (Explain in your own words.)

_____

_____

_____

_____

c. How does this harmonize with, rather than contradict, 12:7-8, which ascribes the victory to Michael and his angels?

_____

_____

_____

_____

d. How do you think 12:11 should affect your life?

_____

_____

_____

_____

_____

War on earth (12:13-17)

5. Explain in your own words what the dragon
   (Satan) does when he is cast to the earth
   (12:13-17).

   _____

   _____

   _____

   _____

6. Why is it important for you to know that when
   he is hurled from Heaven and cannot destroy
   the woman, the dragon makes war against those
   who obey God's commands (12:12,17)?

   _____

   _____

   _____

   _____

7. What important truths about God and His
   people are conveyed in 12:6,14-16?

   _____

   _____

   _____

   _____

Beasts from sea and earth (13:1-18)

In his campaign to make war on the woman's off-spring, the dragon employs two agents: the beast from the sea and the beast from the earth.

Beast coming out of the sea (13:1). The monster from the watery chaos was a familiar symbol of evil in John's time. The Old Testament refers to the stories about Leviathan (Psalm 74:13-14), the dragon of the sea (Isaiah 27:1), Behemoth (Job 40:15), Rahab (Psalm 89:9-10), the sea serpent (Amos 9:3), and the crocodile (Ezekiel 29:3-5). Egypt and its Pharaoh are compared to this sea monster (Isaiah 51:9-10; Ezekiel 29:3-5, 32:2), which represents evil defying God and destined for destruction. In Daniel 7:1-7, the sea monster symbolizes the last nation that rises up against God. Whereas the legends of the dragon and the sea beast overlapped in Jewish and pagan lore, John separates them to distinguish the demonic power (12:3) from the earthly manifestation (13:1).

Some people think the sea beast symbolizes the Roman Empire, which made secular authority divine and persecuted John's contemporaries. Others think it represents political might in every generation that seeks to dominate God's people. Still others think it is the final, great empire or confederation—or the man who runs it—which will claim divinity and attack Christians. All agree that the beast's hallmark is political strength—***horns, crowns, power, throne, great authority*** (13:1-2).

Blasphemous name (13:1). Roman emperors before Domitian were given divine titles after their deaths, but Domitian styled himself *Dominus et Deus noster* ("Our Lord and God"). To call oneself God is the worst blasphemy, and this is what John saw the sea beast doing.

Leopard . . . bear . . . lion (13:2). Daniel had a vision of four beasts: a winged lion that stood up like a man (Daniel 7:4); a bear with three ribs in its mouth (7:5); a winged leopard with four heads (7:6); and a terrifying beast with iron

For Thought and Discussion: Does Satan really control the earth? Why does he have power over the world to give to the beast (13:2)? See Psalm 24:1; Matthew 4:8-10; John 8:44, 12:31; 2 Corinthians 4:4.

97

For Further Study:
What do 1 John
2:18-23 and 2 John 7
say about the Anti-
christ and antichrists?

teeth and many horns (7:7). The beasts represented four successive empires that were going
to arise during the next six centuries (7:17).

John's beast from the sea has characteristics of all four of Daniel's. This empire (and/or
the man who commands it) has all the swift-
ness, brutality, and power of the earlier empires;
it is the epitome of their evil.

Fatal wound . . . healed (Revelation 13:3). The first
Roman emperor to actively persecute Christians,
Nero, killed himself in 68 AD. He was so feared
by even his pagan subjects that a rumor spread
that he was alive in hiding. After several
decades people became convinced that he was
dead, but a prophecy circulated that he would
come back to life and renew his mad terrorizing.
Some interpreters see this myth about Nero as a
type (symbol) of what is or will be true of the
beast:
1. The beast (a world ruler in the last
days) will be slain but will miraculously rise
from the dead.
2. One of the rulers of the great world
empire will be slain, and everyone will think
that the empire is destroyed, but it will rise
again animated with the same malevolent spirit.
3. The evil world order seems to be unkill-
able; although one leader or manifestation is
destroyed, it rears its head again and again.

Another beast (13:11). The beast from the earth is
elsewhere called *the false prophet* (16:13, 19:20,
20:10). He may be:
1. The priests of the emperor cult who
enforced its rules and penalties, making it
impossible for the people of Asia to earn their
livings without participating in the cult.
2. Religious power of every generation
that supports the secular authority in its oppo-
sition to the gospel.
3. An individual false prophet in the last
days who promotes the cult of the individual
antichrist.
4. A group or institution of false prophets
and religious leaders who promote the cult of
the world empire in the last days.

Greek has two words for *another*. One

means "another of the same kind" and the other means "another of a different kind." In Revelation 13:11, the word refers to another beast of the same kind as the first one. In a similar way, Jesus promised that the Holy Spirit would be "another Counselor" like Himself (John 14:16).

A mark (13:16). The kind of mark this is (spiritual, tattoo, ultraviolet, visible, or invisible) is debated, but its purpose is clear: to identify who is and who isn't loyal to the sea beast, so that his enemies can be destroyed.

666 (13:18). In Hebrew and Greek, numbers are indicated by letters (as though a=1, b=2, etc.). It was common to make puns on the numbers that corresponded to people's names. Dozens of attempts have been made to identify the number of the beast with the name of a historical figure. The current favorite is Nero Caesar, but many interpreters think Nero himself simply symbolizes the ultimate antichrist.

The number 7 represented perfection, so 777 would be a great perfection. Second-century Christians observed that *Jesus* in Greek adds up to 888—beyond perfection. Since 666 triply falls short of perfection, it suggests an ironic and demonic contrast with Christ's 888.[5]

For Further Study:
Research marks in the Old Testament.
a. How did God want His people to mark themselves (Genesis 17:9-14, Deuteronomy 6:4-5)?
b. What kind of marks did He forbid, and why (Leviticus 19:28)?
c. How do these references, as well as Ezekiel 9:4, help you understand the good and bad marks in Revelation?

For Further Study:
Investigate the numbers six and 666 in the Old Testament. Whose income was 666 talents? What does the Scripture say about that person?

8. As Christ is God's representative, so the sea beast is Satan's. He is often called the antichrist for this reason: he is a gross parody and opposite of Christ. Below, describe the ways in which the beast distortedly mimicks what Christ is and does.

Christ	the sea beast
"On his head are many crowns" (19:12)	13:1

Christ	the sea beast
"He has a name written on him" (19:12;16)	13:1
He shares the power and Kingdom of God (12:10)	13:2
He "died and came to life again" (2:8); He "had been slain" but stands (5:6)	13:3,14
He "made us to be a kingdom and priests to serve his God and Father" (1:6)	13:4

9. How does the second beast parody Christ, as well as the Holy Spirit who inspires true prophets?

Christ and the Spirit	the earth beast
"a Lamb" with "seven horns and seven eyes" (5:6)	13:11

Christ and the Spirit	the earth beast
7:2-3	13:16-17
11:5-6	13:13
John 16:14	13:12,14-15

10. "Patient endurance" is a theme of Revelation (1:9, 13:10). According to 13:1-18, what will (or do) the saints have to endure patiently?

13:4,8 _____

_____

_____

13:5-6 _____

_____

13:7 _____

_____

13:9 _____

_____

13:14-15 _____

_____

_____

13:16-17 _____

_____

_____

11. Why is it important for you to know this?

_____

_____

_____

_____

12. What is the significance of the fact that the beast "was given" his mouth and his authority for a limited period (13:5,7)? Who do you think gives the beast this power, and why is this important?

_____

_____

_____

_____

Your response

13. What would you say is the overall message of 12:1–13:18?

_____

_____

_____

_____

_____

14. What one insight from 12:1-13:18 currently seems most personally relevant to you?

_____

_____

_____

_____

15. How would you like this to affect your actions and attitudes?

_____

_____

_____

_____

16. What steps can you take to begin putting this into practice?

_____

_____

_____

_____

17. List any questions you have about 12:1-13:18.

_____

_____

_____

_____

For the group

Warm-up. Ask, "How have you experienced Satan's attacks during the past week?" Later, compare your experiences to what John describes in 12:1–13:18. How are your afflictions similar and different?

Worship. Praise God for protecting the woman from the onslaught of the dragon. Praise Him that despite the appearance that the dragon and his beasts have all power and authority on earth, "The kingdom of the world has become the kingdom of our Lord and of his Christ, and he will reign for ever and ever" (11:15). Praise Him that the accuser is in fact defeated, that those who obey God have overcome the accuser "by the blood of the Lamb and by the word of their testimony" (12:11). Ask Him to give you the kind of patient endurance the saints need in the tribulation, the kind that will keep you from shrinking from death (12:11).

Numbers in Revelation

Revelation is full of numbers. One of the questions the book prompts is, "When does a number denote a literal quantity only, when does it have some symbolic meaning, and when is it both literal and symbolic?" Do there just happen to be twenty-four elders and four living creatures, or is there some symbolic significance to these figures?

About 500 BC, a Greek named Pythagoras invented a religious system in which he expressed his ideas in numbers. His number system spread throughout the Eastern world, even among groups who rejected most of his other religious ideas. This number symbolism, along with the practice of adding up the numbers of people's names, became familiar to Jews, pagans, and eventually Christians. Jewish apocalypses are full of it, and there are indications that some of the Old Testament numbers were divinely chosen to convey symbolic meaning to readers familiar with numeric symbols. It is therefore possible, though not certain, that any given number in a book like Revelation may have symbolic meaning. We will let you come to your own conclu-

(continued on page 105)

(continued from page 104)
sions, but here is the Pythagorean system:

One represented "unity, unique, alone, independent, self-existent."

Two "meant companionship, added courage, increased strength, added power, etc."

Three "was the divine number, not only in Judaism, but in other religions as well." (To Christians, of course, three referred to the Holy Trinity.)

Four "referred to . . . the universe or the created world."

Six was an insidious number because it fell short of the perfect seven.

Seven was the sum of three and four, divine and created, spirit and matter. So it symbolized completion, everything.

Ten referred to a complete human being with ten fingers and ten toes—"human completion."

Twelve was three times four, so it represented "organized religion." In the Old Testament, we find twelve tribes of Israel, and in the New we find twelve disciples.[6]

Using this system, some interpreters treat Revelation somewhat as a mathematical puzzle. For instance, 3 is the number of God; 4 stands for the creation or the world; $3 \times 4 = 12$, which means the church (organized religion), through which God works in the world; $12 \times 12 = 144$, the church squared, or the whole church; 10 denotes completeness; $10 \times 10 \times 10 = 1000$, three-dimensional completeness; $12^2 \times 10^3 = 144,000$, "the whole church in all its completeness."[7]

In response to such intricacies, other interpreters reject all symbolism in the numbers. The biblical warrant for the above meanings of 3×4, 10, and so on is less than clear, and many Christians are uncomfortable with the idea of Pythagorean numerology in Scripture. Still, there does seem to be some symbolism in some of the numbers in Revelation. Likely candidates are the sevens, which occur fifty-four times. Another possibility is four—four angels holding back the four winds, and the four living creatures (4:6, 7:1). There were four universally recognized compass points (north, south, east, and west), so

(continued on page 106)

(continued from page 105)

people came to speak of the four corners of the earth and the four winds of heaven. (These were as much figures of speech for the ancients as for us; they were well aware that the earth was round rather than square.) The four living creatures may represent or be the angels of "nature" or "the creation." (Psalm 18:10 says that God travels on a cherub—an angel—and on the wind, so there may be a connection among four winds, four angels, and four creatures.) Or, they may represent God's manifestation of Himself in creation (Romans 1:20)—His majesty, strength, wisdom, and loftiness.

Other figures with possible symbolism are the ten horns, the three and a half years (half of seven), the 144,000, the three and a half days, and 666.

1. *The NIV Study Bible*, page 1939.
2. Beasley-Murray, pages 197-198; Mounce, page 236; Ryrie, pages 77-78.
3. Mounce, page 238, quoting William Hendriksen, *More than Conquerors* (Grand Rapids, Michigan: Baker Book House, 1944), page 195. Some interpreters take the seven and ten literally but the heads and horns symbolically: seven and ten nations or rulers of an empire.
4. Mounce, page 239.
5. Beasley-Murray, pages 219-221.
6. Ray Frank Robbins, "A Book of Imagery, Numbers, and Symbols," *Revelation: Three Viewpoints* (Nashville: Broadman Press, 1977), pages 150-151.
7. Wilcock, page 60. Wilcock cites this example to disagree with it.

REVELATION 14:1-15:8

The Harvest Is Coming

We've seen the cosmic struggle (12:1-17) and its outworking on earth (13:1-18): political and religious might united to crush God's people through economic boycott or outright execution. Things look pretty bleak for believers in chapter 13. But don't despair—chapter 14 offers seven short oracles about the end to encourage us, and chapter 15 introduces the seven last plagues of wrath and justice. As always, the view from Heaven is quite different from appearances on earth.

Read 14:1-15:8, observing what the passage reveals about God.

The Lamb and the 144,000 (14:1-5)

Mount Zion (14:1). Zion was the fortress of Jerusalem, the city David captured and made into his capital. Zion came to be used as a synonym for Jerusalem. The reference here may be to:

1. The earthly Mount Zion. Revelation 14:1-5 may look forward to the earthly millennial kingdom, where Christ and the 144,000 will reign in Jerusalem.

2. The heavenly Mount Zion, as in Hebrews 12:22-24. Revelation 14:1-5 may portray the 144,000 after they have passed through the beasts' persecution and reached glory in the heavenly Kingdom. (In 21:2-3, the heavenly Jerusalem/Zion comes down to the new earth.)

Optional Application: Are you being tempted to commit spiritual adultery, to spend your affections on the world of commerce, politics, and social life rather than on the Lord? If so, how can you overcome this temptation?

Optional Application: Do you "follow the Lamb wherever he goes" (14:4)? What would it mean for you to do this? Be as specific as possible.

144,000 (14:1). These are presumably those of 7:1-8. That is, they are either:
    1. Believing Jews left on earth to witness for Christ during the Great Tribulation when other Christians are raptured.
    2. All the Christians alive during the Great Tribulation.
    3. The whole Church that has passed through earthly tribulation (the whole Church Age between Christ's comings) into glory.
    In any case, the 144,000 have been martyred by the beast and are singing in Heaven.

Defile themselves with women, for they kept themselves pure (14:4). *Pure* is literally "virgins." Some take this literally: the 144,000 are unmarried and celibate men. Others think it is figurative language: they have avoided the "adultery" to which the harlot world city has tempted men and women (17:1-2; compare the defilement of Jezebel in 2:20).
    Remember from 2:14 that adultery was a metaphor for infidelity to Israel's true husband, the Lord (Jeremiah 3:6, Hosea 2:5). When faithful, Israel was called a virgin (2 Kings 19:21).

Firstfruits (14:4). Each year, the first part of Israel's harvest was offered to the Lord in thanksgiving to symbolize that the whole harvest belonged to Him (Leviticus 23:9-14). These are firstfruits in a literal sense. The word is used figuratively for the first convert in an area (Romans 16:5) and the first to rise from the dead (1 Corinthians 15:20). Here in Revelation, the 144,000 may be the first of more people to be redeemed as a result of the tribulation.
    Alternatively, John may mean that the 144,000 are a choice offering to God and the Lamb (premier quality, not necessarily first chronologically). In the Greek translation of the Old Testament current in John's day, the word *aparche* is used to render other kinds of gifts and offerings besides "firstfruits" in the strict sense.[1]

---

1. Explain in your own words the chief characteristics of the redeemed 144,000 (14:4-5).

_____

_____

_____

_____

2. Put a star by each of these traits in which you would like to grow. Talk with God about what you and He might each need to do about this.

3. How does this vision encourage or challenge you?

_____

_____

_____

_____

Three angels and a blessing (14:6-13)

Here are four brief oracles of encouragement and warning.

4. The first of the three angels is flying and proclaiming "the eternal gospel" to the inhabitants of the earth (14:6). What is the eternal gospel (14:7)?

_____

_____

_____

_____

5. Why is this the gospel—the good news?

_____

_____

_____

_____

6. What do the other two angels proclaim?

Optional Application: Could it be said of you, "No lie was found in their mouths" (14:5)? If not, confess and ask God to make this true of you. Meditate on this verse this week, and watch for situations in which you are tempted to distort the truth.

For Thought and Discussion: Why do you think only the 144,000 are able to learn the new song of praise (14:3)?

For Further Study: Compare the gospel in Revelation 14:6-7 to Romans 1:18-25. Why is God's aspect as Creator mentioned in each passage? What other similarities do you find?

**Optional
Application:** What
call for patient endur-
ance (14:12) against
temptation or perse-
cution are you experi-
encing currently? How
can you cultivate
strength to remain
faithful?

14:8 _____

_____

_____

14:9-11 _____

_____

_____

Babylon (14:8). This city in modern Iraq "was the
political, commercial, and religious center of a
world empire. It was noted for its luxury and
moral decadence."[2] Babylon destroyed Judah
and Jerusalem, but many prophets predicted its
downfall in graphic terms (Isaiah 21:9, Jeremiah
51:8). To Israel, Babylon symbolized the epitome of a powerful, evil, worldly city destined for
destruction.

   Some people think John uses the name
Babylon (like Sodom and Egypt in 11:8) to
represent Rome, the center of power and hostil-
ity in his day. Others think he means the world
political and religious system in general. Still
others think Babylon symbolizes the world
government that will be established in the last
days. Some believe Babylon will literally be
rebuilt and become the center of this world
empire.

Cup of his wrath (14:10). God's universal, unending
hatred for sin (this is the meaning of *orge*,
"wrath")[3] is often portrayed as a cup in the Old
Testament (Psalm 75:8, Isaiah 51:17, Jeremiah
25:15). Into this cup is poured full strength ***the
wine of God's fury***—His boiling rage (Greek:
thumos).[4] The suffering coming upon the
beast's worshipers is not the outworking of
impersonal laws of cause-and-effect; it is the
Holy God's passionate response to depravity.

---

7. Why does the announcement of 14:9-11 call for
"patient endurance on the part of the saints"
(14:12)?

_____

_____

_____

8. We read the first beatitude (blessing) in 1:3. Explain in your own words what you think the second beatitude means (14:13).

For Thought and Discussion: a. Why are the dead who die in the Lord from this point on blessed? b. Has this any relevance to you? If so, what is it?

For Further Study: For more illumination of Revelation 14:14-20, see Isaiah 63:3; Joel 3:13; Matthew 13:24-30,36-43; 26:63-64.

_____

_____

_____

_____

9. What lessons for us do the four prophecies of 14:6-13 offer?

_____

_____

_____

_____

The harvest (14:14-20)

Some people take the two visions of 14:14-16 and 14:17-20 as portraying the same event, while others see two related events.

_____

1,600 stadia (14:20). About 180 miles, approximately the length of Palestine north to south.

_____

10. What do you think is the meaning of each of these visions?

14:14-16 _____

_____

111

Optional
Application: What
difference should the
promise of judgment
and wrath against evil
make to your present
life?

14:17-20 _____

Prelude to the last plagues (15:1-8)

Song of Moses (15:3). In Exodus 15:1-18, Moses led Israel in a song to celebrate God's victory over Egypt at the Red Sea. Jews sang this song on Sabbath evenings to rejoice in the deliverance from slavery.[5] The song in Revelation 15:3-4 echoes Moses' song, yet because it is also *the song of the Lamb* it celebrates the fuller deliverance of God's New Testament people.

Tabernacle of the Testimony (15:5). During Israel's desert wandering, the Lord's presence dwelt in a tent or tabernacle. Among sacred objects in the tent was the ark of the covenant (see 11:19), a wooden chest symbolizing God's throne. In the ark were two stone tablets on which the Testimony—the covenant law—was written.

Bowls (15:7). These are ancient drinking bowls. In Isaiah 51:17, the word the NIV translates as "goblet" is literally "bowl of the cup" (NASB margin). In that verse "the goblet [bowl] that makes men stagger" is parallel to "the cup of his wrath." In Isaiah 51:22-23, God promises that the cup or bowl of wrath will be taken out of Israel's hand and put into the hands of her enemies. Thus, it seems that the seven bowls *filled with the wrath of God* (as well as the final punishment in Revelation 20:15) are the cup of wrath that He promised in 14:9-11.[6]

11. Why is it appropriate that the song of the Lamb (15:3-4) is sung just as the seven last plagues

are about to be poured out?

_____

_____

_____

12. What important truths about God are affirmed in 15:1-8? (Record as many observations as you can.)

_____

_____

_____

_____

_____

_____

_____

For Thought and Discussion: Why is it appropriate that those who have been victorious over the beast and his cult are the ones who sing the song of 15:3-4?

Your response

13. What one truth from 14:1-15:8 would you like to concentrate on for application this week?

_____

_____

_____

14. How would you like this insight to affect the way you live?

_____

_____

_____

15. How can you begin acting on this?

_____

_____

_____

113

16. List any questions you have about 14:1-15:8.

_____

_____

For the group

Warm-up. Ask group members how the idea of God's wrath makes them feel. Ask for real, honest answers, not just surface humor or piety. Some people are genuinely uncomfortable with the idea because wrath implies cruelty to them. This is a deep-seated feeling to be faced and prayed about, not ridiculed or applauded. A violent father, for example, can leave a person with a marred perception of God's wrath in his or her heart long after that person has accepted the Christian view intellectually.

Other people are enthusiastic about wrath less because they are righteous than because they are angry, vengeful, or bitter inside. If you find group members unhealthily opposed to or in favor of God's wrath, plan some time at the end of your meeting to pray for clear, holy understanding of divine wrath and judgment. Encourage group members to pray about forgiveness for those people (such as violent fathers) who have helped to distort their understanding of God's justice.

Questions. If you don't find any problems in the area of God's wrath, look for other ways in which 14:1-15:8 should affect how each of you lives now. For instance, how can you as a group grow more like the 144,000?

Worship. Praise God for His holy justice that cannot abide evil. Worship Him as the Creator of everything (14:7), the Vindicator of the righteous (14:3-5,13; 15:2-4), and the Punisher of the wicked (14:8-11). Use 15:3-4 as a springboard to praise.

1. Mounce, pages 270-271.
2. *The NIV Study Bible*, page 1941.
3. Herschel H. Hobbs, "Envisioning God's Ultimate Victory over Evil," *Revelation: Three Viewpoints*, page 119.
4. Hobbs, page 119.
5. *The NIV Study Bible*, page 1942.
6. Beasley-Murray, pages 231-232.

REVELATION 16:1-21

Seven Bowls

Back in 11:14 we heard, "The second woe has passed; the third woe is coming soon." But when the seventh trumpet sounded, it brought a heavenly chorus. Then came vision after vision of the struggle between the Lord and the dragon, culminating in a grim harvest that left the land neck-deep in blood (14:20). From one view God's judgment is a harvest, but from another it is the cup of His wrath (14:10), the cup that the beast and his worshipers must drink. Thus the seals and trumpets are now followed by seven drinking bowl-cups full of wrath. As God promised Israel, so it comes to pass for the world: "If you remain hostile toward me and refuse to listen to me, I will multiply your afflictions seven times over, as your sins deserve" (Leviticus 26:21).

Read 16:1-21 aloud to yourself, carefully and prayerfully.

1. What happens when each of the seven bowls of wrath is poured out?

   16:2 _____

   _____

   16:3 _____

   _____

   16:4 _____

   _____

a. Make a chart with three columns. Label the first column "Plagues of Egypt," the second "Trumpets," and the third "Bowls." In the first column, list the ten plagues of Egypt from Exodus 7:14-11:9. In the second, list the seven trumpet-judgments, and in the third, the bowl-plagues. Use colored markers or another method to mark the similarities.

b. Why do you think God planned the plagues of Egypt to foreshadow those of the last days, or planned the last plagues to imitate the former? (Consider Revelation 15:3-4.)

c. Each of the Egyptian plagues ridiculed an Egyptian god (the Nile god Hopi, the frog goddess Heqt, etc.). How are the bowls directed against the gods of the unbelievers?

d. How is mankind's reaction to the last plagues like Pharaoh's reaction to the plagues of Egypt (Exodus 7:22; 8:15,19)?

16:8-9 _____

_____

16:10-11 _____

_____

16:12-16 _____

_____

_____

16:17-21 _____

_____

_____

There is a similarity between the trumpets and the bowls. "In each series the first four plagues are visited upon the earth, sea, inland waters, and heavenly bodies respectively. The fifth involves darkness and pain (compare 16:10 with 9:2,5-6), and the sixth, enemy hordes from the vicinity of the Euphrates (compare 16:12 with 9:14ff.)."[1] However, the differences are equally significant.

2. The first four trumpet-judgments destroyed a third of the earth (and trees), the sea (and sea creatures), the fresh waters, and the light (8:6-12). How are the bowl-judgments different?

_____

_____

_____

_____

3. a. How is the first plague appropriate for those who have allowed the mark of the beast on their bodies (16:2)?

_____

_____

_____

b. How do the next two plagues fit mankind's crimes (16:4-7)?

_____

_____

_____

_____

4. How do the people respond to the seven plagues (16:9,11,21)?

_____

_____

_____

5. In light of your observations in questions 3 and 4, why are the bowls of wrath, horrible as they are, perfectly just?

_____

_____

_____

_____

_____

Kings from the East (16:12). The **river Euphrates** was the eastern border of the land God granted to Abraham and his descendants (Genesis 15:18, Deuteronomy 1:7-8). It was also the eastern border of the Roman Empire. Israel's enemies often marched from Assyria or Babylonia across the Euphrates, and the Romans were terrified of an invasion from the Parthian Empire, which covered the same region.

Most interpreters agree that the eastern kings are included among, but are not identical with, **the kings of the whole world** (16:14) who are gathered for the last battle at Armageddon.

117

For Thought and Discussion: What do and don't we know about the battle at Armageddon from the information given in Revelation?

For Further Study: Compare Revelation 16:15 to Luke 12:35-48. How can you apply this truth even now?

We are not told what the eastern kings are marching to do, unless it is to fight at Armageddon.

Armageddon (16:16). A Greek transliteration of the Hebrew *Har-Megiddo*, which means "the mountain of Megiddo." Megiddo is the site of an ancient city in central Israel that commanded the pass between the coastal plain and the valley of Esdraelon. Because of its strategic importance, many famous battles have been fought there from 1468 BC to 1917 AD. There is no Mount Megiddo, so *Har-Megiddo* may refer to the nearby hill country, or Megiddo and Mount Carmel (several miles away), or simply the low mound on which Megiddo is built.[2] Some interpreters think the geographical reference to Israel's greatest battlefield is meant to symbolize the final overthrow of evil. Others take it literally.

We are told nothing at all about the battle itself in 16:16. It is generally thought that the battle of 19:17-21 is the same as this one at Armageddon.

6. What are the "evil spirits that look like frogs" (16:13), and what do they do (16:14,16)?

_____

_____

_____

_____

7. The third beatitude is inserted into this brief story (16:15). Why is this blessing so relevant to the context of 16:13-14,16?

_____

_____

_____

_____

_____

8. How is this beatitude relevant to your life?

_____

_____

_____

_____

_____

The great city (16:19). Some people think this is the same as **Babylon** mentioned later in the verse and described at length in 17:1-18:24. Some think it is Jerusalem, others Rome, and others "civilized man . . . ordering his affairs apart from God."[3]

Hailstones (16:21). Hail is often associated with judgment in the Old Testament. It is ironic that the Law prescribed stoning as the punishment for blasphemy (Deuteronomy 13:10, 17:2-5).

Your response

9. What lessons for us can we draw from 16:1-21?

_____

_____

_____

_____

_____

10. Focus on one of these for personal application. How would you like it to affect your actions?

_____

_____

_____

11. What specific steps can you take to begin bringing this about, with God's help?

_____

_____

_____

_____

_____

12. List any questions you have about chapter 16.

_____

_____

_____

_____

For the group

Warm-up. Ask the group, "Do you think that if a (or the) fierce tribulation suddenly fell on your nation, you would be prepared for it? Why or why not? What would you have to do to get prepared?"

Questions. Jesus gave essentially the same warning to His disciples that we find in Revelation 16:15 (Luke 12:35-48), so it seems to apply to us. In fact, part of the reason for studying Revelation is to become motivated to get prepared for tribulation. Instead of debating what Armageddon means, you might concentrate on how you as a group and as individuals can put 16:15 into practice.

Worship. Praise God for His holiness and justice, for ultimately requiting the evil ones as they deserve. Praise Him for His utter abhorrence for sin. Thank Him for the blessing He promises to those who stay awake in the midst of an evil world.

1. Mounce, page 291.
2. Mounce, pages 301-302; Beasley-Murray, pages 245-246.
3. Morris, page 201.

REVELATION 17:1-18:24

The Whore

When the seventh angel poured out his bowl, a massive earthquake shattered "the great city" and collapsed the world's other cities. Through this disaster, "God remembered Babylon the Great and gave her the cup filled with the wine of the fury of his wrath" (16:19). Babylon's fall was promised in 14:8 and glimpsed in 16:19, but it is so important to the message of the Revelation that two chapters are now devoted to it.

Read 17:1-18:24, observing as much as you can about the whore of Babylon.

Great prostitute (17:1). This is her chief characteristic as far as this vision is concerned; her harlotry and adultery are mentioned five times in 17:1-5. Recall from pages 37-38 that both Israel and pagan nations are often called prostitutes because of idolatry—the act of giving oneself to something other than one's true Lord and Husband. *Abominable things* (17:4) or *abominations* (17:5) is a Jewish term for idols.[1]

In Revelation 18 we find that there is a commercial as well as a religious aspect to this city's prostitution.

Many waters (17:1). Babylon was literally built on many waters—the Euphrates River ran through it and a network of canals surrounded it. In John's vision, these waters are symbolic (17:15).

For Thought and Discussion: a. Why do you think idolatry is described as adultery?

b. Why is materialism a form of idolatry?

For Further Study: Study the history and symbolism of Babylon in the Bible: the city's foundation as *Babel*, "gateway to a god" (Genesis 10:8-12, 11:1-9) through the prophets (Isaiah 13:1-14:23, 47:1-15; Jeremiah 20:1-6, 25:1-14, 50:1-51:64) to Revelation. Use a concordance for other references.

121

For Thought and Discussion: What is the point of the way the beast's "resurrection" parodies Christ's (17:8)?

For Thought and Discussion: When you've decided who you think the great prostitute is, then decide who are her prostitute daughters (17:5). For example, are the Protestant churches the daughters of the Roman Catholic Church? Or, who are the daughters of the world system?

Scarlet beast (17:3). The one described in 13:1-10. On the one hand, his *seven heads* (17:3,9) are *seven hills* and *seven kings* (17:9-10). This suggests that the beast is an empire. On the other hand, the beast is identified with the *eighth king* (17:11) who follows the seven, so he seems to be an individual man. Possibly the man epitomizes the spirit of the empire he leads.

Purple and scarlet (17:4). Both dyes were expensive to extract, so they reflected luxury. Purple was the color of royalty, and scarlet represented magnificence.[2]

Mystery (17:5). See the note on 1:20 (page 29). The woman's name is a secret now revealed. Harlots in Rome commonly had their names written on their headbands.[3]

Once was, now is not, and will come (17:8). A parody of the Lamb's name and God's name (1:4,8,18; 2:8; 4:8). The beast's resurrection will impress the unbelieving world, but the beast who will come will also *go to his destruction.*

Seven hills (17:9). Rome was built on seven hills; Latin writers often referred to it as "the city on seven hills." This may imply that the woman is:

1. The Rome of John's day or *Dea Roma*, the goddess-personification of the divine Roman state.

2. The church and empire centered in Rome that will rule the world in the last days. Some say 17:15 suggests that the apostate church embraces many nations and denominations, not just the Catholic Church.

3. The church and empire that will rule the world in the last days. She is portrayed as Rome because for John's readers Rome symbolized world power that claimed divinity and seduced people with her grandeur.

4. "The world as the centre of seduction at any moment of history, particularly during this entire present dispensation."[4] Rome was her manifestation in John's day.

5. The spirit of religiosity and ecclesiasticism, symbolized by Babylon (the root of pagan religion) and Rome.

Among Jews, hills and mountains represented power, so some interpreters think the seven hills are:

1. Seven successive empires from Egypt to Rome (the sixth) to a seventh which may be the Christian empire of Europe or an empire yet to come.

2. The completeness (seven) of strength and solidity, which is a chief characteristic of the seductive world system.

Seven kings (17:10). Here are some explanations:

1. These are seven Roman emperors from Augustus to Domitian (calculations for this vary, since several emperors have to be omitted to make this scheme work).

2. The five who have fallen are not precisely five, but the number simply implies the majority. The sixth is Domitian, the living emperor. The seventh and eighth will come soon. The point is that the Antichrist, who embodies the spirit of the beast-empire and the dragon with Satan behind it, is coming soon.

3. Heads and kings both symbolize authority. When combined with the imagery of hills, they yield a triple symbol of the world's strength.

Ten horns . . . kings (17:12). They may be the kings of the East in 16:12. Some people think they are a league of ten leaders of nations either in the East or in Europe. Others see the "ten" as symbolic of human completeness: all the kings of the world.

---

1. Compare the women of chapters 12 and 17.

chapter 12	chapter 17
their location (12:1,14; 17:3)	

123

Optional Application: Do you find beautiful possessions, fine food, or clothes to be seductive temptations? Would you find the harlot city easy or hard to resist? What should you do about this?

chapter 12	chapter 17
their clothing (12:1, 17:4)	
their offspring (12:5,17; 17:5)	
who loves them (12:6, 17:2-3)	
how they are sustained (12:6,14-16; 17:3,6)	
who hates them (12:13-17, 17:16, 18:8)	

2. What can we learn about the whore's character and identity from what 17:1-18:24 tells us?

character _____

_____

_____

_____

identity _____

_____

_____

_____

_____

For Thought and Discussion: Do you think "the great city" depicted as a harlot in 17:1-18 is the same as "the great city" in 16:19 and/or the one in 11:8? Why or why not?

3. Would you describe the prostitute as attractive, repulsive, or both? Why?

_____

_____

_____

_____

4. Is she someone to be feared, respected, ignored, loved? Why do you think so?

_____

_____

_____

_____

5. The angel's explanation of the "mystery" (secret) of the beast (17:7-17) may leave us more perplexed than before. Still, what do we know about the beast (his identity, character, and actions) from these verses?

identity _____

_____

_____

character _____

_____

_____

_____

actions _____

_____

_____

_____

_____

_____

6. Why do you think the beast who supported the prostitute (17:3) later attacks and destroys her (17:16)? What is the significance of this?

_____

_____

_____

_____

_____

7. What can we learn about God and the Lamb from the angel's words (17:14,17)?

_____

_____

_____

_____

_____

_____

8. Alongside the Lamb (and perhaps fighting with Him?) in His victory over the beast and his followers will be the Lamb's own followers. What is significant about each of His followers' characteristics (17:14)?

called _____

_____

_____

_____

chosen _____

_____

_____

_____

faithful _____

_____

_____

_____

Optional Application: How is the Lamb's victory significant for you personally?

Optional Application: How is it important to you that God is in complete control even when the beast and his followers think they are doing their own will (17:17)?

Optional Application: To what extent could you be described as one of the Lamb's "called, chosen and faithful followers" (17:14)? What are the implications of being called and chosen? How can you act faithfully this week?

9. The beast turns on the woman because he hates her (17:16), but God's purpose is behind even their actions (17:17). For what sins has He condemned her (17:2,6; 18:2-3,7,23-24)?

_____

_____

_____

_____

10. Knowing God's decree, what should His people do, and why should they do this (18:4)?

_____

_____

_____

_____

Optional Application: What warning does the harlot's fate offer us today? How do you think this should affect your actions and priorities?

For Thought and Discussion: a. Why do you think the kings, merchants, and seamen are singled out to mourn the great city's fall?

b. What does this tell you about the city's nature and power base?

11. How do the kings, merchants, and seamen respond to the whore's fall, and why?

kings (18:9-10) _____

_____

_____

_____

_____

merchants (18:11,15-17) _____

_____

_____

_____

_____

seamen (18:17-19) _____

_____

_____

_____

_____

12. In contrast, how should God's people respond, and why (18:20)?

_____

_____

_____

_____

_____

13. What does the harlot's fate tell you about God (18:4-8,20)?

_____

_____

_____

_____

_____

_____

Your response

14. What one insight from 17:1-18:24 would you
    like to take to heart and apply?

_____

_____

_____

_____

15. How would you like this insight to affect your
    priorities, character, and actions?

_____

_____

_____

_____

16. What steps can you take to put this truth into
    practice?

_____

_____

_____

_____

_____

17. List any questions you have about 17:1–18:24.

_____

_____

_____

_____

_____

_____

For the group

Warm-up. Ask, "During the past week, what aspect of the nonChristian world's ways has seemed most tempting to you?"

Questions. This passage contains some of the book's most difficult symbols. Try not to spend too much of your time debating who the seven and ten kings are, and so on. The numbered questions focus on matters that make the passage relevant to your lives regardless of whether the woman is the past Roman Empire, the present world system, or the future world government. If you find yourselves unable to agree on one of these views, treat the vision as though the woman were all three of these. What difference should what you learn about the harlot make to the way you live today?

Worship. Praise God for permitting the harlot her full time of power, for having even her evil manipulator and destroyer under His control, and for assuring you that His is the ultimate victory. Thank Him for enabling you to see the whore in all her true lurid colors.

1. Beasley-Murray, page 252.
2. Mounce, page 309.
3. Beasley-Murray, page 253.
4. Hendriksen, quoted in Morris, page 209.

REVELATION 19:1-21

The Lamb's Victory

Heaven and the saints were called to rejoice over the ruin of Babylon (18:20), and so they do (19:1-5). But the shouts turn from the whore's fall to celebrate the rise of her counterpart, the Bride of the Lamb (19:6-10). Then at last the long-awaited moment arrives: He who "is to come" does come.

Read 19:1-21 to yourself aloud with all the emotion the passage conveys.

Hallelujah! (19:1-10)

Hallelujah (19:1,3,4,6). This word occurs only here in the New Testament. It transliterates a Hebrew word used often in the Psalms. *Halal* means "praise" and *Jah* is Yahweh, Jehovah, "the LORD" in most English translations of the Old Testament. So, *Hallelujah* means "Praise Jah" or "Praise the Lord."[1]

1. How would you describe the mood in 19:1-9?

_____

_____

_____

_____

Optional Application: What difference does it make to you that God's judgments are true and just (19:2), and that the great prostitute will be condemned?

Optional Application: What are the implications for you of the fact that Christ's relationship to the Church is described as a marriage? Do you act as one betrothed to the Lamb? How can this affect your life more deeply?

2. For what deeds and attributes is God praised in these verses?

_____

_____

_____

_____

_____

_____

Wedding (19:7). God told Israel that the nation was His Bride betrothed forever (Hosea 2:19). Jesus described the Kingdom as a marriage feast given by a king for his son (Matthew 22:2). The Apostle Paul said that human marriage is a reflection of the marriage between Christ and the Church (Ephesians 5:32). Some interpreters think the Bride of Revelation 19 is the Church as opposed to Israel; others think she is Israel as opposed to the Church; and others think she is the body of saints of all ages, both Israel and the Church.

Among the Jews, a marriage involved two events, the betrothal and the wedding. After the betrothal ceremony, the couple was considered man and wife and was expected to act faithfully, but the two did not live together. The wedding, which took place some time later, began with a procession to the bride's house. The bride then accompanied the groom and the procession back to his house for the marriage feast. Similarly, the Church (and/or Israel) has been betrothed by faith to the Lamb, but she awaits His return to bring her to His house for the eternal **wedding supper** (Revelation 19:9).[2]

---

3. The great whore was described in lurid detail in 17:1-18:24. We encounter the Bride in 19:7-9 and again in 21:2-22:6. The two have some similarities: both are women, yet both are cities (17:18, 21:2). Write down the differences between the whore and the Bride.

	the whore	the Bride
her relations with the kings of the earth (17:2, 18:9-10, 21:24)		
where she lives (17:3, 21:10)		
what she wears (17:4, 18:16, 19:8)		
the drink she offers (17:4; 22:1,17)		
the mood of her people (17:6; 18:7-10,21-23; 19:7-9; 21:4)		

	the whore	the Bride
her inhabitants (18:2, 21:27)		
her fruit (18:11-14, 22:2)		
her character		
her relationship to God		
other		

134

4. a. To what extent are the Bride's wedding garments earned, and to what extent are they a gift (19:8)?

_____

_____

_____

_____

b. Why is this important?

_____

_____

_____

_____

For Further Study:
Do you think the woman of 12:1-17 is the Bride before the time of her wedding, or are the two women distinct? Explain.

For Further Study:
How does Revelation 19:8 illustrate Philippians 2:12-13?

For Further Study:
Study more about the feast of the Kingdom in Isaiah 25:6-8 and Matthew 26:28-29.

Those who are invited (19:9). Dispensationalists (see page 72) distinguish between the Bride (the Church) and the invited guests (redeemed people who are not part of the Church). According to dispensationalists, redeemed members of Israel who lived before Christ's first coming are not part of the Church/Bride. Likewise, believers converted after the rapture and before the Second Coming (during the Great Tribulation) are not members of the Church/Bride.[3]

Nondispensationalists interpret the rest of Revelation and the New Testament to teach that the Church includes the redeemed of all generations. They say that in imagery such as we find in Revelation and in Jesus' parables (such as Matthew 22:2-14), we should not be surprised to find believers depicted corporately as the Bride and individually as guests at the feast.[4]

5. Explain in your own words the meaning of the fourth beatitude (19:9).

_____

_____

For Thought and Discussion: Why do you think John is tempted to worship the angel who has revealed 17:1-19:9 to him (19:10)?

For Further Study: To understand the robe dipped in blood, see Isaiah 63:1-3 and Revelation 14:14-20.

_____

_____

_____

_____

The testimony of Jesus is the spirit of prophecy (19:10). This is a reason why John should worship God rather than His angelic messenger. Some interpretations are:

　　1. "The study of prophecy should witness to Jesus."[5]

　　2. Jesus' message "is the concern or burden of the Spirit who inspires prophecy." Since Jesus' testimony points people to God, the message of the Spirit through the prophets must also point people to God.[6]

　　3. Jesus' message is the essence (spirit) of what a true prophet proclaims.[7]

　　4. The message about Jesus is the essence of what a true prophet proclaims.

The rider (19:11-21)

6. What characteristics of the rider are mentioned in 19:11-16?

_____

_____

_____

_____

_____

_____

7. Who do you think the rider is, and why?

_____

_____

_____

136

A name . . . that no one knows (19:12). This might
be the name of God, *YHWH*, which the Jews
held to be so holy that they never pronounced it
but said *Adonai* (the Lord) instead. Similarly, it
might be "the name that is above every name"
(Philippians 2:9-11)—"the Lord." It might be
the name John later sees in Revelation 19:16.
Or, it might be a name whose meaning is
beyond the grasp of created beings, as His full
essence is beyond them.

Word of God (19:13). "In Hebrew thought, a word is
not a lifeless sound but an active agent that
achieves the intention of the one who speaks"
(Genesis 1:6-7, Hebrews 4:12).[8]

8. In light of Hebrews 4:12, why is it appropriate
that the rider is called "the Word of God" in
Revelation 19:13? How does this fit the context
of what He is about to do?

_____

_____

_____

_____

_____

9. What impressions of the rider does 19:11-16
leave you with? What do all the symbols tell you
about Him?

_____

_____

_____

_____

_____

For Thought and Discussion: What is your impression of the battle in 19:19-21? Does it seem to be much of a contest? Explain.

For Thought and Discussion: Do you think there is a significance in the fact that the beast and the false prophet are thrown into the lake of fire alive, while the rest are killed (19:20-21)? If so, explain.

10. How is 19:17-19 a grim counterpart to 19:9?

_____

_____

_____

_____

_____

11. What does the rider do in 19:19-21?

_____

_____

_____

_____

_____

_____

Fiery lake of burning sulfur (19:20). A scene of enveloping heat and stench.

Your response

12. What important truths does 19:1-21 offer us today?

_____

_____

_____

_____

_____

_____

_____

138

13. Choose one of these truths to concentrate on for application. How would you like it to affect the way you think and live?

_____

_____

_____

_____

_____

14. What steps can you take to act on this?

_____

_____

_____

_____

_____

15. List any questions you have about 19:1-21.

_____

_____

_____

_____

_____

For the group

Warm-up. Ask what feelings and ideas a wedding feast suggests to the members of your group.

Questions. Draw attention to the shifting moods of this chapter: celebration (19:1-10), majesty (19:11-16), carnage (19:17-21). Focus on the implications for you of the wedding, each aspect of the description of Christ, and the outcome of the final confrontation. How should you live in light of what Revelation 19 says about Christ and His Bride?

Worship. This whole chapter is a fabulous inspiration for worship. The songs of 19:1-8 have been set to music many times. The vision of the rider suggests many attributes of Christ that are worthy of praise. And the defeat of the beast and his followers merits rejoicing.

1. Mounce, page 337.
2. Mounce, page 340.
3. John F. Walvoord, *The Revelation of Jesus Christ* (Chicago: Moody Press, 1966), page 273.
4. Beasley-Murray, page 275; Mounce, page 341.
5. Ryrie, page 112.
6. Beasley-Murray, page 276.
7. Mounce, page 342.
8. Mounce, pages 345-346.

REVELATION 20:1-15

Two Resurrections

Chapter 20 is the focus of more controversy than any other single passage of Revelation. On the variety of views of the millennium, see pages 59-60. Then read 20:1-15 carefully. Observe what the passage actually says, and ask God to reveal the truth of it to you.

1. List the order of things that happen in 20:1-15.

_____

_____

_____

_____

_____

_____

_____

_____

_____

_____

The thousand years (20:1-6)

Thousand years (20:2,4-5). Some interpreters take this as a literal thousand years. Others under-

141

stand it as representing "a long but undetermined period of time."[1]

Many Jews of John's time expected an earthly reign of the Messiah, but the length of it varied. One school saw history as a week of thousand-year "days" (compare Psalm 90:4). As the six days of creation were followed by a day of rest, so there would be six thousand years of human history followed by a thousand years of sabbath-rest in the millennial Kingdom. After that would be the eighth day—the eternal Kingdom. This is how many Christians of the second century AD interpreted Revelation.[2]

They came to life and reigned (20:4). It is not clear whether this includes just the martyrs of the tribulation (***the souls of those who had been beheaded***) or all believers of all generations. It is also not clear whether "those who came to life and reigned" are the same as those on the thrones ***who had been given authority to judge.***

2. What are the four chief traits of the thousand-year period?

20:2-3 _____

_____

20:4 _____

_____

20:4 _____

_____

20:5 _____

_____

3. In what sense are the following true now, and in what sense are they not yet fulfilled?

a. Satan bound (See, for example, Matthew 12:29; Luke 10:17-19, 11:20-22, 22:3; John 12:31; Acts 5:3; 2 Corinthians 4:3-4, 11:14; Ephesians 2:2; Colossians 2:15; 1 Thessalonians 2:18; 1 Peter 5:8.)

true now	not yet fulfilled

For Thought and Discussion: Do you think John's words in 20:4 imply that those who reign are only the martyrs or also the rest of the redeemed? Why? (You might want to compare several translations.)

b. Satan unable to deceive the nations (Ephesians 2:1-3, Colossians 1:13)

true now	not yet fulfilled

c. The witnesses of Jesus reigning (1 Peter 2:9; Revelation 5:10, 6:9-11)

true now	not yet fulfilled

4. What do the following passages suggest to you about the identity of those who sit on the thrones to judge and/or those who are raised to life and reign: Matthew 19:28; Luke 22:30; 1 Corinthians 6:3; Revelation 5:10, 20:4?

_____

_____

_____

_____

_____

For Further Study:
a. Read about Gog
and Magog in Ezekiel
38-39. Observe what
happens before their
battle (chapters
36-37) and after it
(chapters 40-48).
b. What evidence
is there that any of
the battles in Revela-
tion are the same
(16:14-16, 17:12-14,
19:17-21, 20:7-10)?
What evidence is
there that they are
different? Even if they
are different, what do
they have in common?
c. What evidence
is there that the
battle in Revelation
20:7-10 is the same
as or different from
the one described in
Ezekiel?

Satan's doom (20:7-10)

Deceive the nations (20:7). Amillennialists say that
the battle in 20:7-10 is the same as the one in
19:17-21 because the unbelieving nations are
slain in that battle, so they can't be around later
to fight again.

Premillennialists say that while the millennium begins with only believers alive, by the
end of a thousand years generations of children
have grown up and may not all be personally
committed to Christ. The corruption in human
nature has not yet been eradicated. Even without the influence of a depraved world system,
some people grow up rebellious against God and
willing to listen to the tempter. The whole sce-
nario proves that neither the world nor the devil
is the cause of human sin; they merely bring
out the latent potential in man.[3]

Gog and Magog (20:8). Ezekiel 38:1-39:29 describes an attack by "Gog of the land of Magog"
(38:2) upon the restored nation of Israel (the
messianic Kingdom?). Gog is portrayed as a
king leading armies from north of Israel, particularly eastern Asia Minor (modern Turkey). In
Revelation, Gog and Magog symbolize **nations
in the four corners of the earth**, not just the
north, who gather to destroy the messianic
Kingdom.

Judgment (20:11-15)

5. On what basis are the dead judged (20:11-13)?

_____

_____

_____

_____

6. a. Does this include those who have put their
faith in Christ as well as those who have not?
What do Romans 2:6-8, 2 Corinthians 5:10,
and 1 Peter 1:17 say?

144

_____

_____

_____

_____

_____

b. Why is this important for you to know? What
implications does it have for your life now?

_____

_____

_____

_____

_____

_____

**For Thought and
Discussion:** Do you
think the Father, the
Son, or the Triune God
(Father, Son, and
Spirit) is "him who
was seated on" the
throne of judgment
(20:11)? (See Daniel
7:9; Matthew 6:4;
7:22-23; 10:32-33;
Mark 8:38; John
5:22,30; 8:16;
12:47-49; Romans
14:10; 2 Corinthians
5:10; Revelation 4:2.)

7. On what basis will people escape or fail to
escape the lake of fire (Revelation 20:15)?
(Explain in your own words the meaning of
having one's name in the book of life.)

_____

_____

_____

_____

_____

8. Is there a contradiction between your answers
to questions 5 and 7? Why or why not?

_____

_____

_____

_____

_____

Your response

9. How is 20:1-15 personally relevant to you? What important lessons does the chapter teach, and how should it affect your life?

20:1-6 _____

_____

_____

_____

_____

20:7-10 _____

_____

_____

_____

20:11-15 _____

_____

_____

_____

_____

10. What action would you like to take in light of these truths?

_____

_____

_____

_____

_____

11. List any questions you have about chapter 20.

_____

_____

_____

_____

_____

For the group

Read aloud and summarize.

Warm-up. After you've read 20:1-15 and summarized its contents, ask each person to tell the group his or her current beliefs about the millennium. For example, "I think Revelation is saying that Christ will return and establish an earthly reign for a thousand years before the last judgment." Or, "I think that Satan is bound and prevented from deceiving all the nations now, just as he is also leading the tribulation now." Or, "I haven't made up my mind. Such-and-such evidence inclines me to this view, but such-and-such other evidence points me to that view." You'll need an atmosphere of trust to do this, but it will let everyone know each other's perspectives so that you won't be surprised later. Don't let a disorderly argument break out, but wait to discuss 20:1-6 point by point.

Questions. Questions 2 through 4 have great potential for debate. You might want to set time limits for them and enforce the limits firmly. Keep your discussion focused on Scripture as the authority for your opinions. Try to help group members see the biblical rationale behind each view. (Consult a commentary from each viewpoint if necessary.) But don't be afraid of conflict.

Be sure to ask, "So what?" What difference should it make to the way you live if the tribulation and the millennium are now? What if there will be a full thousand-year reign of Christ on the earth in the future?

Don't let a debate of 20:1-6 lead you to neglect 20:7-15. Allow enough time to get a firm grip on what these paragraphs teach and how they should affect your lives in the present.

Worship. Praise God that He has power to bind and loose Satan for His own purposes; even Satan's malevolence is subject to God's greater loving will. Praise God for the promises made to you in chapter 20: (reigning with Jesus), the defeat of Satan, the judgment.

1. *The NIV Study Bible*, page 1948.
2. Beasley-Murray, pages 288-289.
3. Beasley-Murray, page 298; Ryrie, page 116.

REVELATION 21:1-22:6

The New Jerusalem

To end with chapter 20 would have been abrupt, for while 20:7-15 is indeed the end of the world, it leaves us peering out into gaping blackness and silence. What about those who escape the lake of fire, whose names are written in the book of life?

Yet how can God show John in words and pictures what lies beyond human imagination? By transposing echoes from a dozen books of Scripture into a grand key and weaving them together into a triumphant climax for His biblical symphony.

Read 21:1-22:6 aloud to yourself for its overall effect, letting its splendor soak into you. If you are familiar with the Old Testament, listen for echoes of Genesis, Isaiah, Ezekiel, and other books.

(Note: Some interpreters take this as a more-or-less literal description of the Holy City during the earthly millennium, as well as a symbolic description of the Kingdom of eternity.)

No longer any sea (21:1). Since the sea has represented evil—the watery chaos—thus far in Revelation (13:1; compare Daniel 7:3), this statement probably has symbolic meaning in the new earth, as well as a literal one.

Dwelling (21:3). Literally, "tent." This is the word used in the Greek Old Testament for the tabernacle in which God's presence, the pillar of cloud and fire, dwelt (Exodus 40:34-35). The

For Further Study:
Compare Revelation
21:1-22:5 to Genesis
2:4-3:24. What reflec-
tions of Genesis do
you see in Revela-
tion? What is the
point of the echoes
between the two
books?

rabbis called the presence the *Shekinah* (from the Hebrew *shakan*, "to dwell").[1]

1. Revelation 21:3 records the fulfillment of a series of Old Testament prophecies. What does each passage promise?

   Leviticus 26:11-12, Ezekiel 37:27 _____

   _____

   _____

   _____

   Ezekiel 48:35 _____

   _____

   _____

2. Why is this promise so important? What are its implications for you?

   _____

   _____

   _____

3. Revelation 21:4 renews the promise made in Isaiah 25:8 and 1 Corinthians 15:54. What are the implications of this for you?

   _____

   _____

   _____

4. What do you think it means that "To him who is thirsty I will give to drink without cost from the spring of the water of life" (Revelation 21:6)? (*Optional:* See Isaiah 55:1-3; John 4:7-14, 7:37-39; Revelation 22:1.)

   _____

   _____

   _____

Liars (21:8). These are probably not so much those who have told lies as those who have participated in the great lie of the dragon, the beasts, and the whore. Still it may include everyone whose character is bent toward falsehood, who lies persistently (compare 22:15).

5. Why do you think "the cowardly" heads the list of those destined for the fiery lake (21:8)? (*Optional:* See Luke 12:4-12, Revelation 12:11.)

_____

_____

_____

_____

6. Summarize the description of the Holy City in 21:9-21.

_____

_____

_____

_____

For Further Study:
Study the meaning of sonship and inheritance (21:7) in the Old and New Testaments. Find *son, inheritance, heirs,* and *adoption* in a concordance. What does it mean for you that you are God's son or daughter and His heir?

For Further Study:
Study the symbolism of cities from Genesis 4:17 and 11:1-9 through the Psalms (such as 48:1-14) through the prophets (such as Isaiah 23:1-18, 47:1-15, 54:1-17) to the cities of Revelation. Find *city* in a concordance. What are the good and bad aspects of cities?

Twelve (21:12,14). Some call this "the number of the people of God."[2] It figures in every measurement of the city, which is a perfect cube measuring *12,000 stadia* on each side with a wall *144 cubits* (12 x 12) thick (21:16).

The Holy of Holies, the innermost sanctuary of Israel's Temple, was a perfect cube (1 Kings 6:20).

Temple (21:22). As John was writing Revelation, the Jewish Temple had been destroyed for less than thirty years. Jewish writings for that and the succeeding centuries show that the idea of the restored earthly or heavenly Jerusalem without the Temple was inconceivable.[3]

151

For Thought and Discussion: What is signified by the fact that the nations will bring their splendor to the Holy City (21:24,26)?

For Thought and Discussion: What is implied by the fact that the city's gates will never be shut (21:25)? For what reasons does a city shut its gates?

For Thought and Discussion: The new Jerusalem is a city when viewed from the outside (21:1-27) and a garden when viewed from the inside (22:1-5). What is the point? (You might research what the Old Testament has to say about cities and gardens.)

7. What is significant about John not seeing "a temple in the city, because the Lord God Almighty and the Lamb are its temple" (21:22)?

_____

_____

_____

8. a. What other statements are made about "God and the Lamb" (21:23; 22:1,3)?

_____

_____

_____

_____

b. How is it important that God and the Lamb are paired in these verses?

_____

_____

_____

The nations . . . the kings of the earth (21:24,26; 22:2). Some dispensationalists think the nations include those redeemed Gentiles who are not part of the Church and so must live outside the Holy City in the new earth.[4] Most interpreters agree that the verses are to be interpreted spiritually in the eternal Kingdom.

Tree of life (22:2). It is the one tree of Genesis 2:9, 3:22, and at the same time it is the many trees with many kinds of fruit in Ezekiel 47:12.

9. a. What ideas are repeated several times in 21:11,23,25; 22:5?

_____

_____

_____

_____

b. Why are these important enough to be
repeated so often?

_____

_____

_____

See his face (22:4). This was one of the great promises of the Old Testament. Criminals were ban-
ished from the presence of the king (Esther
7:8), but his intimates were allowed to see his
face (Esther 1:14). Moses could not survive seeing God's face (Exodus 33:20,23), but the pure
in heart will (Matthew 5:8, 1 John 3:2).

Your response

10. What important truths have you learned about
the Kingdom of God from 21:1-22:6?

_____

_____

_____

_____

11. How would you like these insights to affect
your priorities, outlook, and actions?

_____

_____

_____

12. What steps could you take along these lines?

_____

_____

_____

For Further Study:
a. On seeing God's
face, see Psalm 11:7,
27:4, 42:2; Isaiah
52:8, 60:1-2; and
Matthew 5:8.
b. Why is the
promise of seeing
God's face important
to you?

**For Thought and
Discussion:** Accord-
ing to 22:3, what will
be the chief occupa-
tion of God's people
in the Kingdom? What
are the implications
of this for our lives
today?

153

13. List any questions you have about 21:1-22:6.

_____

_____

_____

For the group

Read aloud. Ask someone to read 21:1-22:6 with meaning and excitement.

Warm-up. Ask group members to tell how this passage makes them feel.

Questions. The questions in this lesson simply go through the description of the Holy City and help you discover their significance. You can choose just a few to focus on and explore both their meanings and their implications for your lives.

Worship. Take a good length of time to respond to 21:1-22:6 in worship, praising God for what awaits you in His Kingdom.

The End and the Beginning

The final paragraph of C. S. Lewis's book *The Last Battle* is a commentary on the close of Revelation:

"The things that began to happen after that were so great and beautiful that I cannot write them. And for us this is the end of all the stories, and we can most truly say that they all lived happily ever after. But for them it was only the beginning of the real story. All their life in this world and all their adventures in Narnia had only been the cover and the title page: now at last they were beginning Chapter One of the Great Story which no one on earth has read: which goes on for ever: in which every chapter is better than the one before."[5]

---

1. Beasley-Murray, page 311.
2. Beasley-Murray, page 321.
3. Beasley-Murray, pages 326-327.
4. Walvoord, page 327.
5. C. S. Lewis, *The Last Battle* (New York: Macmillan, 1970), page 165.

REVELATION 22:7-21

Epilogue and Review

The Revelation closes in a series of brief prophetic utterances. They may seem random, but they draw together themes threaded throughout the book.

Read 22:7-21 aloud to yourself, watching for repeated ideas.

Jesus is coming (22:7-21)

1. a. What ideas are repeated in 22:7,10,12,20?

_____

_____

_____

_____

_____

   b. What implications do these truths have for your life and your response to Revelation?

_____

_____

_____

_____

155

For Thought and Discussion: Why do you think there is such an emphasis on the authority and reliability of the one who testifies to this book of prophecy (22:6,16,20)?

For Further Study: On Revelation 22:16, see Numbers 24:17 and Isaiah 11:1,10.

Do not seal up (22:10). Daniel was told to "seal up" his book until it was time for it to be fulfilled (Daniel 12:4). Apocalyptists who imitated Daniel and wrote in the names of ancient saints included the same command: the revelation was to be hidden until the end was nigh. (The fiction was that the vision was now unveiled in the time of the real writer, who thought he was living in the end times.)[1] John and his angelic messenger dispense with this fiction: the end is at hand even as John writes; the Church needs his visions immediately.

2. What do you think is the point of 22:11 in context? Explain in your own words.

_____

_____

_____

_____

3. The sixth and seventh beatitudes are in 22:7,14.

a. What does it mean to "keep the words of the prophecy in this book"?

_____

_____

_____

_____

b. Explain who is blessed and what is promised them in 22:14.

_____

_____

_____

_____

156

The Spirit and the bride (22:17). The Holy Spirit and the Church are the two witnesses who testify to the world about Jesus in our time (John 15:26-27). Revelation 22:17 may mean that these two are urging *Whoever is thirsty* to come to the water of life. Or, they may be praying to Christ to come, as He has repeatedly promised He will come (22:7,12,20). Either way, they call *him who hears* (compare 2:7,11,17, etc.) to join them in their cry.

Amen. Come, Lord Jesus (22:20). "Amen" is Hebrew for "so be it" (this affirmation appears in Greek and Hebrew in 1:7). "Come, Lord Jesus" renders into Greek the Aramaic expression *Marana tha* (literally, "O Lord, come"), which became a frequent prayer of the early Church. (*Marana tha* occurs in 1 Corinthians 16:22.)

4. What would you like to take to heart from 22:7-21?

_____

_____

_____

_____

5. What action do you think you should take in light of this?

_____

_____

_____

_____

Review

A review can help you remember not just bits and pieces of Revelation, but the whole sweep of the book. The best way to begin a review is to reread the

Optional Application: a. How does "let him who hears say, 'Come!'" (22:17) apply to you?
b. How can you make this petition a part of your prayers and actions?

Optional Application: Are you thirsty for the water of life, even though you are a Christian? If so, how can you "come" and receive this free gift?

For Further Study: On Revelation 22:18-19, see Deuteronomy 4:2, 12:32.

157

book at one sitting. Don't stop to ponder specific passages, but do watch for (and jot notes about, if you like) threads that tie the book together.

6. Go back through the book and write down a summary or a series of impressions of what you have learned about the following:

God the Father _____

_____

_____

_____

_____

_____

Jesus Christ _____

_____

_____

_____

_____

_____

the Holy Spirit _____

_____

_____

_____

_____

Satan _____

_____

_____

_____

_____

_____

power in the world _____

_____

_____

_____

_____

_____

Kingdom of God (the inheritance of the saints)

_____

_____

_____

_____

_____

_____

the suffering (tribulation) of God's people

_____

_____

_____

_____

_____

_____

the protection of God's people _____

_____

_____

For Thought and Discussion: What have you learned from Revelation about the future?

For Thought and Discussion: What have you learned about the nature of prophecy?

_____

_____

_____

_____

_____

how God wants His people to act in light of the Kingdom, the suffering, and the protection

_____

_____

_____

_____

_____

_____

7. If you had to tell someone in a couple of sentences what Revelation is about, what would you say?

_____

_____

_____

_____

_____

8. What do you think is the most important lesson you have learned from studying Revelation?

_____

_____

_____

_____

_____

9. Have you changed in any ways as a result of studying Revelation? If so, how?

_____

_____

_____

_____

_____

10. Look back through this study guide at questions in which you expressed a desire to make some personal application. Are you satisfied with your follow-through? Are there any areas you would like to continue to concentrate on? If so, describe your plans.

_____

_____

_____

_____

11. Check the end of each lesson to see if any of the questions you had remain unanswered. Write them here. The sources on pages 163-164 may help you find answers. You can also ask another Christian whose biblical understanding you trust.

_____

_____

_____

_____

_____

For the group

Warm-up. Ask everyone to share one way in which your study of Revelation has affected him or her.

Read aloud and summarize 22:7-21.

Questions. You may want to schedule two meetings for this lesson in order to have plenty of time for review. You could spend half of your second meeting evaluating these last few weeks using questions like the ones below. If you need to fit all of this lesson into one meeting, choose just a few of the topics in question 6 to discuss.

Give everyone a chance to answer questions 8 through 11. If possible, let group members answer each other's questions about Revelation, or ask a few people to research answers. It is always best to help the group do things for itself rather than letting it depend on the leader forever.

Some people may feel they have changed little as a result of their study. If so, explore reasons why: How do those members *want* to have changed? Is that what God wants? What has hindered that change? How can your group work on these areas of application together?

Evaluation. Take all or part of a meeting to evaluate how well your group has been meeting members' needs and expectations. Here are some questions you might ask:

What did you learn about small group study from your time in Revelation?
How well did the study guide help you grasp the book?
How did the group discussions help?
What did you like best about your meetings?
What did you like least? What would you change?
How well did you meet the goals you set at your first meeting?
What are the current needs of group members?
What will you do next?

Worship. Thank God for the book of Revelation and for the ways it has affected each of you. Praise Him for all the things you learned about Him. Thank Him for the repeated promise that Jesus is coming soon. Pray for His speedy coming.

Amen. Come Lord Jesus.

1. Beasley-Murray, page 337.

162

STUDY AIDS

For further information on the material covered in this study, consider the following sources. If your local bookstore does not have them, ask the bookstore to order them from the publisher, or find them in a seminary library. Many university and public libraries also have these books.

Commentaries on Revelation

Of the dozens of commentaries on Revelation, we have selected a few that are scholarly, take a high view of the inspiration of Scripture (as opposed to more liberal views) and cover a range of opinions about how to interpret the book. All of these writers would be considered conservative evangelicals.

Beasley-Murray, G. R. *The Book of Revelation* (Eerdmans, 1974).
    Beasley-Murray is a British Baptist scholar and takes a futurist and premillennialist view of Revelation. He is not a dispensationalist and often understands passages symbolically because he sees Revelation as following the methods of apocalyptic in many ways.

Morris, Leon. *The Revelation of St. John* (Eerdmans, 1969).
    Morris is an Australian evangelical scholar. He sees merit in insights from the futurist, idealist, and to some extent the preterist perspectives. He leans toward amillennialism.

Mounce, Robert H. *The Book of Revelation* (Eerdmans, 1977).
    Mounce is also sympathetic to several perspectives, but he is basically futurist and amillennialist.

Ramsay, W. M. *The Letters to the Seven Churches of Asia* (Baker, 1963 [1904]).

This book is not strictly a commentary, but an investigation of the cultural and historical background of chapters 2 and 3. In the late 1800s, most scholars doubted that the seven churches actually existed, and the seven letters were considered to be a literary device. Ramsay did vast and pioneering research to prove that the seven churches actually existed and that each of the letters was crafted to respond to actual situations. Much of his material is echoed in modern commentaries, but serious students might be interested in reading it firsthand.

Ryrie, Charles Caldwell. *Revelation* (Moody Press, 1968).
This is a short, inexpensive paperback that gives a fast overview of a dispensationalist perspective on Revelation. For more exhaustive treatment, see Walvoord.

Walvoord, John F. *The Revelation of Jesus Christ* (Moody Press, 1966).
This is the most thorough and scholarly of the dispensational commentaries on Revelation. As a dispensationalist, he differs from Beasley-Murray in that he believes that the Church will be taken to Heaven ("raptured") before the Great Tribulation. Walvoord and other dispensationalists are also less likely to take statements symbolically and more likely to take them literally than the other commentators in this list.

Wilcock, Michael. *I Saw Heaven Opened* (InterVarsity, 1975).
Wilcock, also from Britain, is largely an idealist and amillennialist. His book focuses more on personal application of Revelation to one's life than most other commentaries—this is its primary focus. Most of Wilcock's insights on application are relevant even if one is neither an idealist nor an amillennialist.

Historical and Background Sources

Bruce, F. F. *New Testament History* (Doubleday, 1980).
A readable history of Herodian kings, Roman governors, philosophical schools, Jewish sects, Jesus, the early Jerusalem church, Paul, and early Gentile Christianity. Well-documented with footnotes for the serious student, but the notes do not intrude.

Harrison, E. F. *Introduction to the New Testament* (Eerdmans, 1971).
History from Alexander the Great—who made Greek culture dominant in the biblical world—through philosophies, pagan and Jewish religions, Jesus' ministry and teaching (the weakest section), and the spread of Christianity. Very good maps and photographs of the land, art, and architecture of New Testament times.

Packer, James I., Merrill C. Tenney, William White, Jr. *The Bible Almanac* (Thomas Nelson, 1980).

One of the most accessible handbooks of the people of the Bible and how they lived. Many photos and illustrations liven an already readable text.

Concordances, Dictionaries, and Handbooks

A *concordance* lists words of the Bible alphabetically along with each verse in which the word appears. It lets you do your own word studies. An *exhaustive* concordance lists every word used in a given translation, while an *abridged* or *complete* concordance omits either some words, some occurrences of the word, or both.

The two best exhaustive concordances are *Strong's Exhaustive Concordance* and *Young's Analytical Concordance to the Bible*. Both are available based on the King James Version of the Bible and the New American Standard Bible. *Strong's* has an index by which you can find out which Greek or Hebrew word is used in a given English verse. *Young's* breaks up each English word it translates. However, neither concordance requires knowledge of the original language.

Among other good, less expensive concordances, *Cruden's Complete Concordance* is keyed to the King James and Revised Versions, and *The NIV Complete Concordance* is keyed to the New International Version. These include all references to every word included, but they omit "minor" words. They also lack indexes to the original languages.

A **Bible dictionary** or **Bible encyclopedia** alphabetically lists articles about people, places, doctrines, important words, customs, and geography of the Bible.

The New Bible Dictionary, edited by J. D. Douglas, F. F. Bruce, J. I. Packer, N. Hillyer, D. Guthrie, A. R. Millard, and D. J. Wiseman (Tyndale, 1982) is more comprehensive than most dictionaries. Its 1300 pages include quantities of information along with excellent maps, charts, diagrams, and an index for cross-referencing.

Unger's Bible Dictionary by Merrill F. Unger (Moody, 1979) is equally good and is available in an inexpensive paperback edition.

The Zondervan Pictorial Encyclopedia edited by Merrill C. Tenney (Zondervan, 1975, 1976) is excellent and exhaustive, and is being revised and updated in the 1980s. However, its five 1000-page volumes are a financial investment, so all but very serious students may prefer to use it at a church, public, college, or seminary library.

Unlike a Bible dictionary in the above sense, *Vine's Expository Dictionary of New Testament Words* by W. E. Vine (various publishers) alphabetically lists major words used in the King James Version and defines each New Testament Greek word that KJV translates with that English word. *Vine's* lists verse references where that Greek word appears, so that you can do your own cross-references and word studies without knowing any Greek.

Vine's is a good basic book for beginners, but it is much less complete than other Greek helps for English speakers. More serious students might prefer *The New International Dictionary of New Testament Theology*, edited by Colin Brown (Zondervan), or *The Theological Dictionary of the New Testament* by Gerhard Kittel and Gerhard Friedrich, abridged in one volume by Geoffrey W. Bromiley (Eerdmans).

A *Bible atlas* can be a great aid to understanding what is going on in a book of the Bible and how geography affected events. Here is a list of a few good choices:

The Macmillan Atlas by Yohanan Aharoni and Michael Avi-Yonah (Macmillan, 1968, 1977) contains 264 maps, 89 photos, and 12 graphics. The many maps of individual events portray battles, movements of people, and changing boundaries in detail.

The New Bible Atlas by J. J. Bimson and J. P. Kane (Tyndale, 1985) has 73 maps, 34 photos, and 34 graphics. Its evangelical perspective, concise and helpful text, and excellent research make it a very useful purchase, but its greatest strength is its outstanding graphics, such as cross-sections of the Dead Sea.

The Bible Mapbook by Simon Jenkins (Lion, 1984) is much shorter and less expensive than most other atlases, so it offers a good first taste of the usefulness of maps. It contains 91 simple maps, very little text, and 20 graphics. Some of the graphics are computer-generated and intriguing.

The Moody Atlas of Bible Lands by Barry J. Beitzel (Moody, 1984) is scholarly, very evangelical, and full of theological text, indexes, and references. This admirable reference work will be too deep and costly for some, but Beitzel shows vividly how God prepared the land of Israel perfectly for the acts of salvation He was going to accomplish in it.

A *handbook* of biblical customs can also be useful. Some good ones are *Today's Handbook of Bible Times and Customs* by William L. Coleman (Bethany, 1984) and the less detailed *Daily Life in Bible Times* (Nelson, 1982).

For Small Group Leaders

The Small Group Leader's Handbook by Steve Barker et al. (InterVarsity, 1982).
Written by an InterVarsity small group with college students primarily in mind. It includes information on small group dynamics and how to lead in light of them, and many ideas for worship, building community, and outreach. It has a good chapter on doing inductive Bible study.

Getting Together: A Guide for Good Groups by Em Griffin (InterVarsity, 1982).
Applies to all kinds of groups, not just Bible studies. From his own experience, Griffin draws deep insights into why people join groups;

how people relate to each other; and principles of leadership, decision making, and discussions. It is fun to read, but its 229 pages will take more time than the above book.

You Can Start a Bible Study Group by Gladys Hunt (Harold Shaw, 1984).
Builds on Hunt's thirty years of experience leading groups. This book is wonderfully focused on God's enabling. It is both clear and applicable for Bible study groups of all kinds.

How to Build a Small Groups Ministry by Neal F. McBride (NavPress, 1994).
This hands-on workbook for pastors and lay leaders includes everything you need to know to develop a plan that fits your unique church. Through basic principles, case studies, and worksheets, McBride leads you through twelve logical steps for organizing and administering a small groups ministry.

How to Lead Small Groups by Neal F. McBride (NavPress, 1990).
Covers leadership skills for all kinds of small groups—Bible study, fellowship, task, and support groups. Filled with step-by-step guidance and practical exercises to help you grasp the critical aspects of small group leadership and dynamics.

DJ Plus, a special section in *Discipleship Journal* (NavPress, bimonthly).
Unique. Three pages of this feature are packed with practical ideas for small groups. Writers discuss what they are currently doing as small group members and leaders. To subscribe, write to Subscription Services, Post Office Box 54470, Boulder, Colorado 80323-4470.

Bible Study Methods

Braga, James. *How to Study the Bible* (Multnomah, 1982).
Clear chapters on a variety of approaches to Bible study: synthetic, geographical, cultural, historical, doctrinal, practical, and so on. Designed to help the ordinary person without seminary training to use these approaches.

Fee, Gordon, and Douglas Stuart. *How to Read the Bible For All Its Worth* (Zondervan, 1982).
After explaining in general what interpretation (exegesis) and application (hermneneutics) are, Fee and Stuart offer chapters on interpreting and applying the different kinds of writing in the Bible: Epistles, Gospels, Old Testament Law, Old Testament narrative, the Prophets, Psalms, Wisdom, and Revelation. Fee and Stuart also suggest good commentaries on each biblical book. They write as evangelical scholars who personally recognize Scripture as God's Word for their daily lives.

Jensen, Irving L. *Independent Bible Study* (Moody, 1963), and *Enjoy Your Bible* (Moody, 1962).
The former is a comprehensive introduction to the inductive Bible study method, especially the use of synthetic charts. The latter is a simpler introduction to the subject.

Titles in the LifeChange series: